World Architecture

William George

World Architecture

BLANDFORD PRESS

Poole   Dorset

First published in the U.K. 1980
Copyright © 1980 Blandford Press Ltd,
Link House, West Street,
Poole, Dorset, BH15 1LL

ISBN 0 7137 0953 7 (Hardback edition)
ISBN 0 7137 1089 6 (Paperback edition)

Phototypeset in Monophoto Apollo
by Oliver Burridge and Co. Ltd

Printed in Hong Kong by South China Printing Co.

Contents

Acknowledgements

The publishers gratefully acknowledge the following for permission to reproduce colour and black and white illustrations (numbers refer to colour plates): Alan Hutchison Library, 2, 3, 4, 11, 16, 18, 20, 27, 32, 37, 47, 48, 51, 52, 57, 58, 60, 64; Peter Baker Photography, 10, 35, 38, 39; British Tourist Authority, 9, 44, 50, pp. 54, 163; Iraqui Cultural Centre, 23; French Government Tourist Office, 46, p. 138; Netherlands National Tourist Office, 45, p. 144; Japan National Tourist Organisation, 36, p. 37; Irish Tourist Board, 54; Australian Tourist Commission, 63; Scottish Tourist Board, 53; National Tourist Organisation of Greece, 5, 6, 8; Italian State Tourist Department 30; Egyptian State Tourist Administration, p. 16; Cyprus Tourism Organisation, pp. 26, 51; Foto Enit Roma, p. 30; Government of India Tourist Office, pp. 34, 47; Turkish Tourism and Information Office, p. 42; Iranian Tourist Office, p. 45; Belgian National Tourist Office, p. 122; Danish Tourist Board, p. 8; Austrian National Tourist Office, p. 146.

The author would also like to acknowledge the following for supplying colour illustrations: Mark Knowles Library; M. Colleridge; Foto Albino Grapelli; Keith Fowler; Picture Press International; Yale, Marsh & Smith; Mike Yonge; Simmons Smith Associates; The Islamic Library, Ankara; J. M. Mukherji, Photography, New Delhi; R. J. Sant-Manduca Collection; Lux Pics; James Campbell-Johnston; Margaret Pendlebury; Bateman Photo Library; M. Sanchez; H. N. Rudolfsky; the Ridley Collection.

1
What is Architecture?

Architecture may be described as the art of designing and creating beautiful, durable and useful buildings. First used in about 1563, the word 'architecture' was derived from the Latin *architectura*, which itself came from the Greek *architekton* which meant 'master builder'. Structures which are built with only stability and strength in addition to usefulness in mind may be described as works of engineering. It is only when the idea of building beautifully in conjunction with strength and utility is introduced that the science of building becomes the art of architecture. There have always been many builders, but not so many master builders; it is the latter to whom we refer when we speak of architects and architecture.

In very early times, when man lived in caves, he had no need for architecture. Even when he lived in a tent, wigwam, rude shelter or other primitive building such structures were merely buildings and in no sense could be described as architecture. Man's early attempts at building were intended for his personal protection. He wanted shelter from the elements and from his enemies. As he became more expert he introduced strength and stability into his constructions, both in his workmanship and in the material he used. The latter was largely dictated by the geological and climatic conditions of his environment. Geographical conditions had a considerable effect on the growth of civilization in every country. They also greatly influenced the character of the people and played no small part in developing intellect and culture.

Architecture itself has always been greatly influenced by geological, geographical and climatic conditions; and religious, social, political and historical influences have also had a considerable effect on architecture and its development. Architecture does in fact touch upon every aspect of the life of man. After providing for his shelter and protection, there came the urge to aim higher and to satisfy other desires. Usefulness alone was not enough. As time went on, the idea of beauty crept in and builders vied with each other to embellish and adorn their structures.

Grundtvig's Church, Copenhagen. Consecrated in 1940, the church is built in yellow stone in a style inspired by the typical Danish village church.

Religion has always been closely associated with the development of architecture and has drawn on the best master builders for the creation of temples, tombs, cathedrals and churches. In the very early days of man's building aspirations, he built a special place for his god, which

8

until then had lived in the same structure as him, and as he progressed in his development so he introduced ornamental beauty and elegance into his work. When a people was highly religious, its craftsmen put into the building of temples their very best work; nothing was too good or expensive. When a people believed in a future life, great lengths were taken in the building of tombs to protect the dead. Those who were more interested in their present existence concentrated more on the building of their houses than on their temples or tombs, and produced places of great magnificence and grandeur.

Social, political and historical changes also had a considerable influence on architecture and its development. In some instances large numbers of subject populations have been available for huge works, as have also prisoners taken in war as slaves. Vast undertakings were often attempted when forced labour was readily available. Conquest and occupation of a primitive country resulted in the introduction into that country of ideas and styles which had already developed in the country of the conquerors. Quite often existing structures were pulled down and new ones built on their foundations. It was fairly usual for them to be only partly demolished and parts of a later style or more advanced type to be added. So, when we examine, for example, an ancient church, we find perhaps that it was built on the foundations of a more ancient temple and that very often the building consists of parts built in different styles and periods.

The intended use of a building will govern the type of structure to be erected, and architecture itself represents the attempt to satisfy the need for that building in an artistic and lasting manner. A covering or roof will be required which must be supported by walls or by pillars, the tops of which must be joined together by ties of some sort. The sides of openings for doors and windows must similarly be tied, otherwise the supports of the roof are likely to fall.

The space between pillars or bridging openings such as doors and windows can be tied by a flat beam referred to as a lintel, or by constructing a round arch or a pointed arch. Quite often the materials available dictated the method used. The lintel was the least strong of these methods, and had no elegance or beauty. Prehistoric peoples used it, the Egyptians employed it, the Assyrians developed it and the Greeks perfected it.

The round arch was first employed by the Egyptians. Later, the Assyrians and then the Etruscans made use of it. The Romans used it in conjunction with the lintel of the Greeks and developed the Roman style. The Assyrians used the round arch before the rise of Greek artistry, as did the Etruscans who built it with a keystone.

The arch greatly exceeds the lintel in strength. The latter is limited to being constructed with one piece, whereas the former consists of a number of pieces. The pointed arch is a stronger form than the round arch. The pointed or Gothic style made it possible to have larger window openings and more of them.

When corbelling was used in construction, successive pieces projecting over the one immediately below from both sides of the space were finally joined when the top pieces met or were tied with a single block. Corbelling the walls of a structure was an early means of building a roof or cover supported only by the walls. A method of bridging wide spans which is a feature of modern structures is the truss, which is made up of several pieces of metal or wood which form a compound beam.

Finally, a method employed by the Romans involved the hardening or setting of materials into a structural unit. Concrete was employed, which was moulded into the required forms and strengthened by rods or wires embedded in the concrete. This method is generally referred to as reinforced concrete. Although it is largely used in purely engineering construction, its use in architecture is now commonplace.

Each of these methods represented a big step forward in the development of architecture. It was a gradual process and many types of people in many places played their part in the development from primitive to civilized architecture. The techniques employed were often dictated by the materials or the methods commonly used in those areas, and those methods played a large part in the development of particular architectural styles.

The stone columns used to support the ceilings of tombs at Beni-Hasan in Middle Egypt, which were cut in the solid rock, show a marked resemblance to those of the Doric order developed by the Greeks. Although the Assyrians had knowledge of them, they did not use columns for supports. The Persians, on the other hand, who had large stocks of stone available, made extensive use of columns. They had probably taken the idea of columns from the Egyptians. The Greeks also made great use of columns and beams. Their columns placed together in numbers were a distinctive feature, as their stone or marble lintels were necessarily of limited length. It was the pointed arch which finally made wide openings or gaps between supports possible. As civilization and skill developed, the early efforts were modified and artistically improved.

2
Prehistoric and Primitive

Prehistoric architecture and primitive architecture are often regarded as one and the same thing. It is a mistake, however, to think that the terms are synonymous, for prehistoric architecture in many cases is extremely sophisticated, showing a profound knowledge of structural necessities and of the engineering skills required to erect buildings.

Primitive architecture, on the other hand, is as its name implies basic and primitive in outlook and in the materials used in the construction of simple structures. From the architectural point of view, primitive architecture is a misnomer, for the simple and rude structures erected by tribal and primitive societies can rarely be classified in architectural terms. The majority of tribal dwellings, wherever they be found, are usually constructed of the simplest and most readily available materials, such as straw, grass, wood or palm-leaves. In construction, they normally consist of a simple wooden skeleton (if large enough) and are covered with the materials cited. Rarely do they exceed a single cell or room, though this may in some cases be of very large dimensions. Occasionally, primitive dwellings may be supported on stilts; at the other extreme they may simply be a covering of grass or palm-leaves over a sunken pit. Only rarely has primitive architecture influenced any major architectural traditions of the world. An example of one of these rare occasions where a simple palm-leaf hut influenced a highly sophisticated architectural style can be seen in some of the mogul architecture in India. Some buildings, including the Red Forts at Agra and Delhi, had pavilions which were constructed imitating in marble the simple Bengali fishermen's hut. Mogul architecture also incorporates other features in marble and sandstone from the Hindu architectural tradition which were normally constructed in wood. Occasionally, tribal societies excelled themselves and sought to produce lasting architectural edifices, such as the magnificent stone ruins of Zimbabwe, in Africa.

Builders of prehistoric times were not content simply to use perishable materials such as grass or palm-leaves, but strove to erect permanent edifices in which to live (though this was somewhat rare), to worship or to bury their dead. To these ends, they utilized wood and eventually stone. Prehistoric lithic architectural traditions can, on the whole, be divided into the *cyclopean* tradition and the *megalithic* tradition. In the former, structures were built normally without mortar or other binding agents by placing large boulders or naturally fashioned stones one on top of the other, so that they interlocked in the same manner as a modern dry stone wall. The stones were generally large, sometimes weighing as much as a ton, and certainly many hundredweights, hence the term cyclopean. Megalithic structures are quite different in as much as they are constructed from large stone slabs, shaped either naturally or by man. These slabs normally weigh many tons, and are rarely less than a few hundredweights. The method of construction is simply to butt together stone slabs adjacent to each other to form a wall, although in some of the more sophisticated structures, such as in Malta, walls may be formed by placing some slabs at 'T' junctions to each other in order to provide a more stable structure.

Several methods of roofing cyclopean and megalithic structures were employed. In some cases, roofing was simple, consisting either of a wooden framework on which matting, grass or palm-leaves were used as thatch, or of corbelling. In the latter, slabs were placed on the megalithic uprights in such a way that they over-hung the interior. The same technique was employed by cyclopean builders. Each layer would overlap the layer before and would form a primitive type of dome which was capped by a slab, or, in the case of cyclopean techniques, come to a natural closing point.

The techniques described above were employed by many civilizations and cultures at different times throughout the world. Highly sophisticated megalithic structures are found in Scandinavia, France, Germany, Italy, Spain, Malta, Great Britain, Ireland, India and even Japan. Cyclopean structures are also found in countries throughout the world, including Crete, Greece and even South America, and some buildings often incorporate both methods of construction. For instance, in Malta, the interiors of some of the megalithic temples, especially that of Ggantija on the Island of Gozo, are constructed in the cyclopean tradition, but the external walls are megalithic. The whole structure is bound together with a rubble filling between the inner and outer walls.

Prehistoric man constructed buildings using these techniques mainly for the purpose of worship and for burying the dead. Such was the motivation of magic and the belief in fertility and after-life that he invested his energy not in building comfortable dwellings for the time spent on earth but in propitiating the natural forces that governed his life and affected his crops and animals, and in ensuring an existence after death. In Britain, megalithic structures tend to be collective tombs and they are covered by mounds of earth. These are known as long barrows. Similar barrows are found in Europe. Simple burial chambers consisting of three orthostats and a capping stone, also covered with a mound of earth, though in many cases now eroded, are called dolmens. These, too, are found in many parts of the world. Sophisticated temples are found in a few places of the world, the most spectacular being in Malta. Some of these structures are decorated with engravings and reliefs of a highly developed symbolic art.

In addition to structures, megaliths were also employed for circles and linear alignments such as Stonehenge in Britain and Carnac in France. These appear to be an elaborate form of astronomical calendar.

Another form of prehistoric archaeological tradition which must be mentioned before leaving the subject is that of the cave and cliff dwelling. These tend only to be found in areas where conditions were conducive to their construction. Some of the most elaborate to be excavated were found by the American Indians in North Mexico and Arizona.

3
Egyptian

Egypt, one of the most ancient of civilizations, had an abundance of building stone, and, because of the importance placed by the Egyptians on their life after death, their great architectural works were erected as tombs and temples. They were massive in size and yet so perfectly constructed that many of them still survive. Although the Pyramids were built as royal tombs and go back to at least 3500 B.C., because of their size and construction they must be the result of a vast experience in architecture. They certainly could not have been the first architectural works to have been undertaken in Egypt. Although there are over a hundred throughout Egypt, the three which are larger than the others are at Giza, a suburb of Cairo, and belong to the fourth dynasty. The base of the Great Pyramid measures 764 feet (233 m) on one side and the height is 482 feet (147 m). It was built of limestone and inside it were three main chambers with a number of passages constructed with granite and limestone. The two smaller pyramids were 454 feet (138 m) and 218 feet (66 m) high; but the method of construction was the same. Each of the pyramids contained a burial chamber and each had a temple nearby, few of which have survived. The Pyramids represented only a small part of the architectural activities of the ancient Egyptians; they built temples of considerable size in which the priests and others lived; these were centres of activity as well as temples.

Generally, the approach was by way of an avenue guarded by stone carved sphinxes. Near the entrance was a number of single columns. The façade consisted of two towers or pylons with walls sloping inwards from the bases. The walls were decorated with sculptures and hieroglyphics and topped by a cornice with a roll and bead moulding. The doorway between the towers was similarly decorated. Going through the courtyard into the great hall, one met with a tremendous wealth of ornament which made the exterior look comparatively plain. There were elaborate carvings and rows of lofty columns supporting the roof. The capitals of the columns either represented the lotus, sometimes closed and sometimes opened, or the leaves of the palm tree. It has been said that the Egyptian builders were at their peak when they constructed their temples.

The kings of ancient Egypt devoted themselves to the construction of new temples, and to beautifying and adorning existing ones, rather than to their palaces. They had plentiful supplies of stone and the forced labour of many thousands of slaves, and during the course of one lifetime were able to construct a vast amount of gigantic architecture. On the exterior of the walls were coloured reliefs extolling the virtues and glory of the king, for the benefit of his people, whereas on the interior the virtues and worship of the gods were repeatedly represented. Some of these temples were extremely large. The temple of Amen-Ra at Karnak, for example, is the largest; it is 1215 feet (370 m) long and 376 feet (115 m) wide. It is entered from the Hypostyle Hall which itself measures 340 feet by 170 feet (104 m × 52 m) and has 16 rows comprising 134 columns supporting the stone roof. The columns in the centre are 70 feet (21 m) high and are nearly 12 feet (4 m) in diameter. They have inverted bell capitals. The other columns are smaller and lower, as the roof they support is lower than that over the centre aisles. They have lotus bud capitals. Stone grated windows joining the higher roof to the lower roofs light up the interior.

There are two other styles of temple. The grotto temples are gigantic achievements which reproduce in the solid rock the features of structural temples. The peripheral temples are of only moderate size. These very graceful buildings served as chapels and consisted mainly of a small chamber surrounded by columns.

Egyptian architecture, in the main, was based on the use of the lintel. Its beauty largely depended on painted pictures and carved reliefs. Those roofs which were too wide for single lintels had to be supported by columns, which in some instances because of their height, size, number and decorations were most impressive. Simple columns were plain and square, but others more elaborate were carved with lotus stalks, flowers, or heads. The columns were rarely more than six diameters high. Generally, the shafts were tapered upwards. They were round or sometimes clustered and were adorned with five main types of capital: the inverted bell, the clustered lotus bud, the plain lotus bud, the palm capital and the Hathor-headed, which had four heads of Hathor surrounded by a shrine. These types were richly decorated by the architects. Every part of a column was decorated in rich colours. Sometimes lotus leaves or petals were wrapped around the lower widening part of the shaft, which elsewhere was covered with bands of carved

The temple of Amen-Ra at Karnak, Luxor, Egypt.

hieroglyphics and pictures. The capital also was covered with carvings and paintings of lotus leaves or flowers or stalks of papyrus and lotus.

The lintels, which were of great size, were quite plain. When they were visible from the outside they were capped by a cornice, which was often covered with coloured flutings and hieroglyphics. Mouldings very seldom appeared in Egyptian architecture.

The use of colour was most important in the decoration of Egyptian buildings. In the glare of the sun outside, or the dimness of the light inside, sculpture or reliefs without colour would not have shown up to the same extent. The walls and columns were covered with coloured pictures and carvings, as also were the ceilings, which were decorated in the same manner but mainly with symbolic forms. The ornaments, not the paintings, were symbolical. The symbol of the sun flying to conquer the night was represented by a disc with outstretched wings, which was usually placed over the gateway. The ceiling was often decorated with vultures, or stars on a blue background. Outside, the unbroken walls were covered with historical pictures.

So far we have dealt with tombs and temples because these were of such great importance to the Egyptians. As they spent so much of their time outdoors, the buildings in which they lived were not so important to them. In the main, they were constructed only of brick or timber, and so there are very few remains left for us to examine. Pictures on the walls of temples and tombs suggest that the walls of their houses were probably made of wooden frames filled in with wooden panels or bricks. The larger ones might have had wooden ceilings supported by wooden posts. Such structures were quite simple. In a number of instances ground plans can be discerned in ruins but there are no traces remaining of any parts of the superstructure.

The artistic architectural development of Egypt can be broadly divided into five eras.

The *Old Empire* covered the first ten dynasties which ruled from Memphis from about 3400 to 2160 B.C. The *Middle Empire* of the eleventh and twelfth dynasties ruled from Thebes until 1788 B.C., when invasions etc. interrupted artistic development for two centuries. The Middle Empire was actually the First Theban Monarchy.

The *Second Theban Monarchy* was probably the greatest period of Egyptian history; it covered the eighteenth, nineteenth and part of the twentieth dynasties. It was an age of giant constructions and also of expansion by conquest, and extended from 1588 to 1150 B.C.

Then came the *Late New Kingdom and Saitic Periods* which covered the dynasties up to and including the twenty-sixth, ruling from Tanis, Bubastis and Sais. The New Empire Period consisted of the period of the Second Theban Monarchy and the Late New Kingdom and Saitic Periods, minus the period of Persian conquest.

A great number of tombs known as mastabas were also built by the Egyptians. These were rectangular in shape with inclined sides and flat ceilings, were usually constructed of stone or brick, and always faced the east. Divided into three parts, they each had a chapel, a secret inner chamber and a well which led down deep into the mummy chamber. It is thought that the pyramid shape was evolved from that of the mastabas, of which there are three at Giza.

There are also a number of tombs cut in solid rock, whose entrances face the east. The ceilings, which are curved, are supported by columns formed by cutting away the rock, probably examples of the first use of columns. Some of these tombs penetrated several hundreds of feet into the rock and they were often decorated with coloured reliefs and ornaments.

At Giza there is also a large sculpture carved from rock. It represents a lion with a human head and is 70 feet (21 m) long and 66 feet (20 m) high. Close to it is a temple which, although called the Sphinx Temple, is now believed to be associated with the second pyramid and also the Persian conquest. These periods covered the years from 1150 to 324 B.C.

Then came the *Revival* covering the Ptolemaic, Macedonian and Roman periods of rule from 324 B.C. to A.D. 330.

4
Near Eastern

The Chaldean, Assyrian and Persian Empires ruled this part of the world in turn. The Valley of the Tigris and Euphrates had a civilization almost as old as that of the Nile. A scarcity of timber and a lack of stone suitable for building, except some limestone, together with the flat terrain, had a considerable influence on the form and concept of the architecture. The three main periods of art in this area may be described as the *Chaldean* (about 3000 to 1250 B.C.), the *Assyrian* (1250 to 606 B.C.) and the *Babylonian* (606 to 538 B.C.). The empire then fell to the Persians who ruled it until 331 B.C.

The Chaldeans, and later the Assyrians, found very little material for their buildings except clay which they used extensively. Therefore much of their architecture was of bricks which were fixed together at first with bitumen, which was available to them, and later with mortar. The Assyrians found stone to the east and used some stone as slabs which were carved in relief with sculptured pictures. Often, for decoration, bricks were worked with figures which were painted, then glazed and fired.

The Persians tended to copy the architecture of the Assyrians; as they had more plentiful supplies of stone and marble available, they were able to make advances on the work of the Assyrians.

These peoples constructed huge platforms or mounds on which they built their temples and palaces. These mounds, which were largely constructed of earth, were faced with bricks and were from 20 to 50 feet (6–15 m) high. The general scarcity of stone and wood finally resulted in the development of the arch and arch tunnelling. The Assyrians did not use columns for supports, although their sculptured stone slabs depict buildings with columns and capitals, which appear to be the forerunners of the Greek Ionic and Corinthian columns. The Persians used stone columns. Perhaps they copied the Egyptians in this, but their columns were not so large. They never attained in their architecture the accuracy of the Egyptians, whose work was near perfection. They borrowed from the art of the Assyrians and evolved a style of architecture in stone and in wood which was derived from the wooden prototypes of Persia itself and Central Asia. Their columns were used internally in hypostyle halls and externally to form porches. These halls were of great size; the Hall of Xerxes at Persepolis had an area of 100,000 square feet (9290 m²), whereas the Hall at Karnak was only nearly half that size. The Persian columns were forked, and were used with wooden architraves which made wider spaces possible than if stone was used. For example, the Karnak Hall had 134 columns, whereas almost the same area in the Hall of Xerxes needed only 36 columns. The shafts were finely fluted and slender and produced a very different effect from those of the Egyptians which were painted and carved. In the Hall of Xerxes the columns were over 66 feet (20 m) high and 6 feet (1.8 m) in diameter.

The doors and windows of the Persians had banded trims and cornices which were very Egyptian, and their portals were flanked with Assyrian-type winged bull monsters built up with courses of stone and not carved out from single blocks.

The Persian Empire under the Achaemenid dynasty, which ruled until 331 B.C., included present-day Iran, Egypt, Libya, Iraq, Afghanistan and part of Turkistan. The flat-roofed palaces with their stone columns at Persepolis, Susa and Pasargadae and tombs at Naksh-i-Roustam, Persepolis and Pasargadae date from this period.

No other peoples of this area developed an individual style which produced outstanding examples of architecture, although perhaps the Cypriots, Phoenicians and Lycians played an intermediate part between the art of the Egyptians and the Assyrians and that of the Greeks. The Greeks might have learned a little about sculpture and pottery from the Cypriots. The Phoenicians, who were traders, distributed the goods of Egypt and Assyria throughout the Mediterranean area and contributed largely to the spread of ideas. They copied the Egyptians and the Assyrians in producing similar goods which they decorated in a similar fashion, but they left little of architectural interest.

The Lycians evolved a style of tomb which could have had some influence on Persian and Ionian builders. For the most part, the tombs were cut into solid rock, although some were free-standing and were mounted on a high base. All of these tombs convey the idea that they are stone copies of wooden structures. The roofs are gabled and have a banded architrave, and a cornice. Sometimes they have projecting eaves with rounded rafters. Several have porches which have primitive Ionian type columns, which may have been forerunners of those perfected by the Ionic Greeks.

The Hebrews never seemed to have developed a style of architecture of their own, but they absorbed ideas from all with whom they came into contact. Near Jerusalem there are tombs of various periods, some of which were carved in the rock, whereas some were structural. The greatest example of Jewish architecture was the Temple at Jerusalem, which was first built by King Solomon in 1012 B.C. and combined Egyptian ideas with Phoenician and Assyrian details and workmanship. It was built on a gigantic raised platform, which was doubled in size in 18 B.C. when it was extended by a terrace wall with stones 22 feet (6.7 m) in length; one even was 40 feet (12 m) long. The Wailing Wall is part of this terrace. When the Temple was rebuilt by Herod, the old design was reproduced in part and the porch of Solomon was retained. It was reconstructed in white marble and embellished with gilding, and was truly one of the most magnificent structures of ancient architecture.

Two of the city gates of Jerusalem had carved arches which bore carved acanthus leaves similar to those carved on the frames of the openings of the rock-cut tombs, with carvings of other plants and grapes. These could have been the prototypes of Byzantine ornamental decoration.

5
Greece—Pre-Hellenic

The Hellenic orders of Greek architecture which have played such an important part in the development of western architecture were, in fact, not the first great architectural traditions to develop in the Peloponnese; for, over one thousand years before the first great Greek Hellenic buildings were constructed, a magnificent architectural tradition existed on the Island of Crete, and at Mycenae on the mainland. The buildings of the Minoan and Mycenaean civilizations were quite different from those of Hellenic Greece.

The Mycenaean civilization was discovered in 1876 by Heinrich Schliemann, and the Minoan civilization by Sir Arthur Evans, excavating at Knossos in Crete in 1901. At both sites a remarkable architecture was discovered. At Mycenae, Schliemann discovered the ruins of elaborate shaft graves with corbelled roofs, the most famous being the treasury of Atreus, which was constructed in about 1185 B.C. Another superb architectural feature of the citadel of Mycenae which was constructed of massive masonry blocks is the 'Lion Gate', built about 1200 B.C. On Crete, Sir Arthur Evans discovered the ruins of an elaborate palace at Knossos. Later, other sprawling palaces were discovered at Phaistos, Gournia, Zakro, and Mallia. These palaces consisted of hundreds of small inter-connecting rooms constructed on several levels. Many of the rooms were decorated with beautiful frescoes. From as early as the beginning of the middle Minoan period, that is 1900 B.C., the Minoan buildings were constructed with good ashlar masonry, and some buildings were faced with gypsum and the interior of some rooms plastered. Frescoe painting did not, however, occur before the end of the Minoan period. The buildings had many sophisticated architectural features including an ingenious system of drainage and water supply. In fact, the architecture could almost be described as modern. In addition to the palaces, the Minoan civilization had elaborate tholos tombs which, like the Mycenaean, also had corbelled roofs.

There is little evidence to suggest any influence of the Mycenaean and Minoan architecture on the architecture of later Greece.

6
Greece—Hellenic

The Dorians and the Ionians, who gave their names to the systems of design known as the Doric and Ionic orders, developed the architecture of classical Greece. In Egypt the column was mainly used as an internal support, whereas in Greece it was an external feature which gave the structure an imposing appearance. Columns became indispensable to the Greeks and they made great use of them in their public squares, temple enclosures and gateways. Each of the two types of column had its distinctive shaft, capital, base, mouldings and ornaments which constituted the 'order'.

The column of the Doric order tapered towards the capital. Its height was between four and six-and-a-half times its smallest diameter. The shaft was fluted with about sixteen to twenty channels. The capital had a large convex moulding which supported the upper square cap.

The Ionic column was more slender and ornate than the Doric, and depended more on carving for its decoration. It was usually eight to ten diameters high. The shaft usually had twenty-four flutings. Its base was frequently ornamented with figures in relief, and the capital had spiral-shaped scrolls on either side.

A third order, the Corinthian, developed out of the Ionic and was more ornate still. It was often used in conjunction with either the Doric or Ionic order. It had a very distinctive capital which consisted of an inverted bell surmounted by a spiral form and surrounded by rows of acanthus leaves.

Using these orders as their main decoration, the Greeks built up a magnificent and imposing architecture. They were outstanding in the structure of their temples, which were intended mainly to enshrine the statue of their deity. They were not intended to accommodate large numbers of worshippers nor to exclude all but a select few from secret rites performed only by the priests or the king. The statue was enshrined in a fairly large chamber to which the public had access through a columned porchway. Beyond the chamber was a smaller one which acted as a depository for offerings; beyond this was a rear porch. The whole structure was impressively surrounded by a colonnade, and was covered by a single gabled roof. The temple architects aimed at beauty and perfection; they used stone and/or marble according to availability. Usually the roofs were of wood, decorated at the ends with sculpture. Terracotta or marble tiles were used to cover the roofs. Interior columns were used to give support to the roofs when chambers were too wide to be spanned by single beams.

The Greeks had great skill and delicacy in their cutting and working of stone, and they appear never to have been daunted by any dimension which may have been needed to achieve their object. The architraves in the Propylaea at Athens, for example, were each made of two or three lintels placed side by side. The longest measured 17 feet 7 inches by 3 feet 10 inches by 2 feet 4 inches (5.4 m × 1.2 m × 0.7 m). In some really gigantic temples much larger blocks were used and they were cut and fitted perfectly.

Greek architecture during the Hellenic Period may be roughly divided into six periods: the Archaic Period, the Transitional Period, the Periclean Age, the Alexandrian Period, the Decadent Period and the Roman Period.

The *Archaic Period* extended from about 650 to 500 B.C., during which the Doric order was used almost exclusively. The columns were heavy in proportion and coarse in their finish. Temples of this era included the Temple of Apollo at Syracuse, and the Heraeum at Olympia. Generally, limestone or marble was used and the designs were obviously based on earlier constructions of timber.

The *Transitional Period*, which covered the short time up to about 460 B.C., showed a considerable improvement in the standard of design, ornament and workmanship in the architecture of the temples. There was also a great improvement in sculpture, and the development of the Ionic order made a considerable difference. During this period three temples were constructed which deserve mention—the Aphaea Temple on the Island of Aegina, the Temple of Zeus at Olympia, and the Temple of Hera Lakinia at Agrigentum in Sicily. The Temple of Zeus was built of a coarse conglomerate which was finished with stucco and decorated with sculpture. It was the scene of the rites which attended the Olympic Games.

The end of the Persian wars marked the end of the Transitional Period and the beginning of the *Periclean Age*. The enthusiasm and wealth resulting from the defeat of the invaders brought with them a desire to reconstruct the old monuments as well as to build new ones. The

Acropolis at Athens was crowned by the Parthenon, which is acknowledged to be outstanding in its design and execution. It was considered a masterpiece also for the beauty of its sculpture and was constructed as a shrine for a statue of Athena Parthenos which was 40 feet (12 m) high. To the north of the Parthenon was the Erechtheum, an example of the Attic-Ionic style of architecture. There was a smaller monument of the Ionic order to the south-west—the temple to Nike Apteros.

The gateway to the Acropolis, the Propylaea, made use of the Doric and Ionic orders together. The front and rear façades were Doric, but the centre passageway passed between two rows of Ionic columns. Its execution was perfect and it was indeed a worthy gateway to the other magnificent architecture of the Acropolis. The Doric and Ionic orders were also combined in the Temple of Apollo Epicurius at Phigalaea. South of the Acropolis was the Theseion, a temple to Vulcan. It was constructed of marble and had all the refinements of the Periclean Age, but not as much sculptural decoration as the Parthenon. In Athens, also, was the Ionic temple on the Ilissus. Doric temples of this era included the Temple of Athena at Rhamnus, and the temples of Themis and Nemesis at Argos.

The *Alexandrian Period* lasted from about 400 to 300 B.C. A number of wars destroyed the peace for about seventy-five years. Athens lost her supremacy in these wars, from which she never fully recovered. Just as the earlier age called for artistic perfection, splendour was the aim at this time. The Corinthian capital began to appear. The Temple of Apollo Didymaeus at Miletus was perhaps the largest of all the huge edifices built at this time; its measurements were 366 feet by 163 feet (112 m × 50 m). The temple of Artemis at Ephesus was 342 feet by 163 feet (104 m × 50 m). The most lavish expenditure was incurred on temples, shrines and tombs, and the workmanship was exquisite.

After the decline of the magnificence of the Alexandrian period, Greek art also declined. The Stoa of Attalus and the Tower of the Winds at Athens were examples of the works of the *Decadent Period*, 300 to 100 B.C., which were relatively weak and lifeless. There were, however, some structures which are worthy of mention. The Altar at Pergamon executed in Ionic style was an imposing and masterly piece of architecture, as also was the Ionic Temple to Zeus at Aizanoi with its elegant frieze decoration of acanthus leaves and scrolls.

Finally, we come to the *Roman Period*, which covered the years from about 100 B.C. to A.D. 200, when Roman domination and influence were spreading over Greece and as a consequence structures erected were partly Roman and partly Greek in concept and in detail. At Athens the Temple of Zeus at Olympia was started in about 170 B.C. and not finished until A.D. 130. It measured 354 feet by 135 feet (108 m × 41 m) and its columns were 57 feet (17 m) high, with perfect Corinthian capitals. Also belonging to the Roman period were the Arch of Hadrian, A.D. 117, and the Odeon of Regilla, A.D. 143.

We have mentioned only a few outstanding monuments other than temples created by the Greeks. Their gateways were, of course, very impressive and so were their colonnades. The Greek theatres were, in the main, cut from rocky hillsides, the seats being steps of stone or marble which swept round the sloped excavation.

There were also buildings created as stadia or hippodromes for races, exercise, bathing and other amusements. Many of them also had semi-circular tiers of seats for spectators.

Tombs included the famous Mausoleum at Halicarnassus, erected in 354 B.C. It was in the Ionic style, measured 80 feet by 100 feet (24 m × 30 m), was built on a base 50 feet (15 m) high and was surrounded by thirty-six Ionic columns.

The temple of Apollo at Kourion, Cyprus.

7
Roman

The Romans were very practical people and great organizers. The Greeks evolved the Doric, Ionic and Corinthian orders of architecture; the Romans used and developed these, together with the Tuscan, which was a variation of the Doric, and the Composite, which was a combination of the upper part of the Ionic with the lower part of the Corinthian.

From an early date, Dorians occupied the southern part of Italy and Sicily, and they built magnificent examples of Doric art. The Phoenicians, as traders, brought with them goods and ideas from other countries.

The Etruscans occupied Etruria in about 1000 B.C. This area south of Florence and north of Rome must have had a considerable influence on the new architecture centred on Rome, which arose from the Roman use and development of the Greek orders. The absorption of the Etruscans by the Romans involved the addition of a people who were to play a leading part in this development.

The Romans put engineering to work in the service of architecture, which they fitted to their own particular requirements. They built magnificent arches, amphitheatres, villas, baths, temples and basilicas, all of which bore the stamp of Roman origin, although they made considerable use of artists and artisans of many races. Roman architecture adapted itself to a wide variety of materials. The arch and the vault became the basis of their system of architecture, and they organized the construction of their buildings so that they could make the maximum use of unskilled labour, so arranging the design of their decorative adornments that workmen of only ordinary skill could do the work in a satisfactory manner. They developed their planning to perfection and achieved a great variety of combinations.

In the closing years of the Republic, the only art the Romans had was Etruscan. With the Empire, Roman architecture took on its own characteristic form. The conquest of the Greek states gave rise to imperial splendour which replaced the primitive Etruscan style. The Greek conquests brought in vast artistic spoils and large numbers of Greek artists.

Corinthian columns of the Roman Maison Carrée at Nîmes in France.

The conquerors pillaging the marble colonnades, temples, theatres and gateways had the ambition to have the same impressive architecture, and they adopted, adapted and applied Greek ideas to their own requirements. The use of columns and arches together gave rise to a system of architecture which became just as Roman as the Doric and Ionic orders were Greek.

The Romans kept the Etruscan column with its simple entablature. They modified the Doric and Ionic, and developed the Corinthian order to make it completely independent of the others. They gradually evolved standard proportions with growing experience until rules of proportion were finally laid down.

In each of the orders the base was given a height of half a diameter taken at the lower part of the shaft. The shaft tapered about one-sixth of its base diameter towards the capital. The entablature was about one-quarter of the height of the whole column.

The Tuscan was basically an Etruscan Doric; the column was seven diameters high. The Doric was made eight diameters high. The shaft was either smooth or fluted and had a simple base on a square plinth. The Doric was only changed a little, principally in mouldings and decoration of the capital. The column was about nine diameters high. The Corinthian order had a column of ten diameters, a special base was designed and elaborate carvings enriched the cornice. It was so changed as to become essentially a Roman order, and it did in fact become the normal and favourite order for their architecture.

The Romans preferred monolithic shafts to superimposed drums when constructing a column. With such shafts they omitted the fluting, and, when the stone used was hard or semi-precious, they polished the shaft to bring out the colour of the stone. These polished shafts were often very large and were used extensively.

The Romans also mounted their columns on pedestals to give them greater height without increasing the size of the column and its entablature. Another Roman innovation was the use of columns as wall decorations or buttresses. Usually the column projected over half its diameter from the wall, and was so built that the wall became part of it.

Wherever possible, the Romans substituted wooden ceilings with brick, stone or concrete. Actually it was the Etruscans who brought the building of vaulting to Europe, and the Romans commonly used three types of vault: the dome, the barrel vault and the groined vault. The dome, as in Hadrian's Pantheon, was supported on a circular wall built up from the ground. The barrel vault was usually semi-cylindrical, and

Atrium of the house of Marcus Lucretius, Pompeii.

The house of the 'cenacolo', Pompeii.

was generally used to cover oblong halls or corridors. The groined vault was formed by the joining of two barrel vaults at right angles.

Generally speaking, the Romans made the smaller vaults of concrete cast into moulds of rough boards. The larger ones often had a skeleton of ribs made of brick to support the concrete. They made the vault just as important as the arch and the column. Roman vaulted architecture called for enormous weights to be supported by piers and buttresses, and great use was made of clay lime and pozzolana, which made an excellent cement. Where brick and concrete were not readily available, stone was used. Walls had the inner and outer faces built of cut stone and the space between was filled with rubble and cement.

The Romans made use of carved ornament in the decoration of their architecture. They used the acanthus leaf and foliage, often combined with natural forms. Grotesque masks, dolphins, griffins, infants, wreaths, festoons, ribbons, eagles etc. were all common features of their relief carving. They made much use of panelling and moulded plaster for their interior decoration. They also employed mosaic made up of numerous cubes of stone or glass as floor or wall decoration. Thin slabs of rare or richly coloured marble were often used as veneer on walls.

In the fourth century A.D., when the population was about one million, it is estimated that there were at least four hundred temples in Rome. Nevertheless, they also built structures in which to live, tombs, bridges and other works of utility. Their palaces and houses anticipated the comforts of present-day living, particularly in their plumbing, heating, utensils and furniture.

8
Oriental

Oriental architecture is the complete antithesis of occidental architecture. It would, however, be a mistake to generalize the architectural styles of such a vast area; for India, Japan and Tibet have each produced their own distinctive styles which have evolved and changed over many centuries. The inspiration of much of Oriental architecture, however, is to be found in the rich architectural heritage of India. The buildings of this vast sub-continent are both varied and impressive. Indeed, some of the greatest temples of India must be looked upon as some of the major architectural wonders of the world. Unlike western architecture, they are highly symbolic and illustrate the Indian preoccupation with metaphysical matters.

India has had a tradition of civil and architectural engineering extending back over nearly 4,000 years. Although utilitarian in character, the ruins of the Indus valley culture at Mohenjodaro and Harrapa in N. W. India illustrate the grand nature of the pre-Arian architectural tradition of India.

The Arian tradition can trace its origins in India as far back as the time of the Mauryan empire. At that time, a number of Persian craftsmen emigrated to India after the fall of the Achaemenid Empire. At Pataliputra, near present-day Patna, in Bihar, the remains of a large hall was excavated in 1912. The hall, which contained over eighty pillars, each with a high lustrous polish, shows very strong Persian influence, and recalls a Persian Diwan or Apadana—audience hall. The hall was erected during the reign of the Emperor Chandragupta. Later, during the reign of Asoka, Chandragupta's grandson, Persian influence shows a marked imprint on Indian architectural thought. Although the influence may have been Persian, the symbolism was entirely Buddhist. It was during this period that the three basic types of Buddhist structures had their origins—the Stupa or relic mound, the Chaityas or temple halls, and the Viharas or monasteries.

It must be remembered that these architectural styles did not originate in isolation but were influenced by Vedic (Hindu) traditions and built by craftsmen used to interpreting Hindu ideals. Thus, to varying degrees, Indian architecture, although expressing Buddhist, Jain or Hindu sentiments, is very similar in concept and only different in detail.

Some of the greatest architecture that India has produced was Buddhist in inspiration. The famous stupa at Sanchi, which is 120 feet (37 m) in diameter and 56 feet (17 m) high, is a superb example of Buddhist architecture. It consists of a hemispherical mound surrounded by a richly carved stone fence, with gateways of elaborate workmanship, each with three sculptured lintels across the carved uprights. One of these gateways has an inscription which dates it to the first half of the second century B.C. Another marvellous stupa was found at Bharhut in Central India. The stupa, which dates to the Sunga period, was discovered in 1873 by General Cunningham. The sculptures which decorate the stupa show Persian influence. The site of Bodh Gaya, where the Buddha obtained Enlightenment, is also an excellent example of early Indian architecture, although it is not a stupa, but resembles more the tower-like form of some Hindu temples. A fine example of a stupa of the Gupta period can be found at Sarnath, near Varanasi, in the Deer Park, where the Buddha preached his first sermon.

Chaitya Halls are mainly carved out of the solid rock, but preserve architectural features which give an idea of the appearance of much of the architecture of the time. The earliest, at Karli, dates roughly from about 78 B.C. The latest date to the post-Gupta period, i.e. A.D. 600, and later. In form, they consist of a broad knave which ends in an apse, and two narrow side-aisles. A small stupa or dagoba was placed in the centre of the apse. The façade of the Chaitya caves were carved to resemble free-standing structures. Chaityas preserve features of architecture probably executed in wood, which have long since perished. Some of the finest examples are found at Ellora and Ajanta. As well as Buddhist halls, there are also Jain and Hindu structures at both these sites.

One of the most impressive of all Hindu temples can be found at Ellora. Known as the Kailasa temple, this massive structure has been hewn entirely out of the living rock, to form a free-standing temple with external and internal architectural features. The building is a perfect illustration of Hindu thought and its application to architecture, in that it symbolizes in the multitude of sculptures married to architectural form the holy mountain Kailasa. At this stage, one must point out a major difference between a Chaitya hall and the Hindu temple. The Hindu temple simply houses the image of the deity, and does not accommodate a congregation. Worship is directed towards the building which

The Great Stupa, Sanchi, India.

contains the image, and is essentially carried out outside the buildings.
Entry is not necessary. Chaitya halls were halls for the congregation to
worship within.

Buddhist Viharas were mainly constructed of wood, and have long
since perished. Stone examples can, however, be found in Gandhara
(N. W. India) especially at the site of Jamalgiri and Takht-i-Bhai. The
plan is a simple one, in which three or four courts are surrounded by
cells. In the centre of one court is a platform for an altar or shrine. In
addition to these sites, there are rock-cut chaityas at Ajanta and Bagh,
which date from the fifth to the seventh centuries A.D.

The Jain style is similar to the Buddhist, but is generally far more
elaborate. Although these structures are often confused with the Buddhist structures, especially with the similarities in iconography, they can
usually be distinguished by the fact that icons of Jain Tirthankara are
nude, whereas figures of the Buddha and Bodhisattvas are always
clothed.

34

Perhaps the finest and earliest example of Jain architecture can be found at Mount Abu. Built in 1032 by Vimalah Sah, it principally consists of a court measuring 140 × 90 feet (43 m × 27 m), surrounded by cells and a double colonnade. In the centre is a shrine containing an icon of the Jain Tirthankara Mahavira, which has a high spire/tower or sikhra. In front of the shrine is an imposing columnar porch which is cruciform in plan. Eight columns separate a dome which is covered with sculptured figures, the total effect of which is one of remarkable dignity and splendour. The so-called Victory Towers are another feature of Jain architecture; examples of these can be found at Chittore in Rajasthan. These towers provide an excellent illustration of the characteristics of much Hindu and Jain architecture by the superimposition of different planes, the combination of vertical and horizontal lines, openings, niches and rich ornamentation, which is integral to the structure, conveying a wild rhythm of life.

It is difficult to give a general description of Hindu architectural styles, as they differ widely owing to their geographical position. It is best perhaps to list certain groups of temples which will illustrate the variety and the identity of the overall concept of Hindu architecture.

The northern style is best illustrated by the temples at Khajuraho, especially Kandarya Mahadeo, which is the most notable and certainly the most splendid example of Northern Hindu architecture. The building is impressive; a strong and lofty lower level supports an extraordinary mass of roofs, covering six open porches, antechamber and a hypostyle hall rising in a pyramidal mass until it reaches the vimana or sikhra 116 feet (35 m) high which covers the shrine. The entire building is covered by successive layers of sculpture, which is integral to the structure. It has a vigour and grandeur unusual for its size (it is relatively small). Other temples of the Khajuraho group are equally distinctive and impressive.

The oldest examples of the style are found on Orissa at Bhubaneswar and Konarak. The temple of the Sun at Konarak, otherwise known as the 'Black Pagoda', is a magnificent building, the product of the collective imagination of a most artistic people. Constructed in the form of a giant Chariot of the Sun, it is a symphony of sculpture and architectural form.

The central style is exemplified by the buildings of the Chalukyas (eleventh to thirteenth centuries) of the Deccan. The most interesting of these are the highly ornate, almost lace-like temples at Halebid and Belur. The plans are star-shaped whereas the vimana is pyramidal. The temples give an overall impression of extraordinary richness and beauty, with the surface being broken up by rectangular projections, so arranged as to give an impression of buildings of greater dimensions than their true size. Some are double temples, as at Halebid, while others are even triple in plan. A noticeable feature of the style is the deeply cut stratification of the lower part of the temples, each band or stratum bearing a distinct frieze of animals, figures or ornament, carved with masterly skill.

The southern style of the Dravidians (dating around the twelfth century) is in marked contrast to that of the Deccan. Dravidian temples are not simple structures but aggregations of buildings of varied size and form covering extensive areas enclosed by walls and entered through doors made by imposing lofty gates called *gopuras*. The early architecture of the Pallavas is far more impressive and majestic. The best examples are the Raths or scale models at Mahaballipuram. These superb mini-structures are in fact architectural models carved out of single pieces of rock. The stone temple at the same site is also of great architectural interest.

Indian architectural ideas played a major role in the orient, for they spread not only south to Sri Lanka and south-east to Indonesia, Bali, and Cambodia but also north to Nepal, and east to China and Japan.

While the tradition that spread to south-east Asia was purely lithic, that which spread to Nepal, China and Japan was a separate but equally important tradition, based on wood. Most Indian examples have long since perished, but a style which dates around the sixth century survived, and was modified in Nepal, Tibet, and played no small part in China.

The lithic architecture of China and Japan can in no way compare with the rich and flamboyant architecture of India, for, although the Chinese possessed considerable decorative skill and mechanical ingenuity, these are the only qualities which show in their buildings. Most buildings in China and Japan were constructed of wood. Notable exceptions are the ceramic tower of Nanking, built in 1412, and destroyed during a rebellion in 1850 (it was a 236 feet (72 m) high pagoda riveted with porcelain tiles), and the Temple of Heaven in Peking.

Apart from ingenious framing and bracketing of the carpentry, the most striking feature of Chinese buildings is their broad-spreading tiled roof. These invariably slope downward in a curve, and the tiling, with its hip-ridges and finials, adds materially to the general effect. Colour and gilding are freely used.

Japanese architecture is far more refined than that of the Chinese, and their approach more original. They too have concentrated on wooden architecture, though for the practical reason of coping with the ever-present danger of earthquakes. Wood is used for palaces and temples. Japanese buildings have similar roofs to Chinese, but the overall effect of Japanese buildings is one of greater refinement and delicacy.

In Japanese architecture, natural beauty enhances man-made forms.

9
Early Christian

Just as many races built up the outstanding art of Rome, so too Christianity enlisted under one common purpose a large number of peoples whose cultures were widely different. The Emperor Constantine gave official recognition to Christianity in A.D. 313. Until that time Christians had been forced to meet in secret. They had earlier found that basilica-type buildings were well suited to the requirements of their worship and they began to build in imitation of them. In A.D. 330 Constantine moved his capital from Rome to Byzantium, which became known as Constantinople. He built a basilica in his new capital and splendid churches in Bethlehem and Jerusalem. He had a peculiar preference for circular buildings.

A number of basilicas were built in Rome after A.D. 330. Generally, they had a broad and lofty nave which was separated from the aisles at the side by rows of Corinthian columns. The aisles were usually only about half the width of the nave, as the wooden roof and ceiling above them was only half the height of that above the nave. Above the columns flanking the nave rose a wall pierced with windows which supported the massive trusses of the roof over the nave. Sometimes the timber of the roof was bare, but in other instances it was covered by a panelled ceiling, carved, gilded and painted. At the far end of the nave was the sanctuary or apse with seats for the priests, and also the altar.

In front of the basilica was the atrium or forecourt surrounded by an arcade which formed a porch. The exteriors of the basilicas were very plain, but the interiors were richly decorated, much use being made of small cubes of glass built up into coloured mosaics. As rituals became more elaborate, and with growing wealth, the furniture and other church equipment became more highly decorative and assumed more architectural importance. A high canopy was built over the altar, and pulpits were built on either side. A large rectangular space was kept for the choir in front of the platform for the clergy. In the early basilicas, adjoining were the baptistry and the tomb of the saint, usually circular buildings; later these were replaced by the font in the church and the confessional under the altar.

Constantine built two basilicas in Rome, one dedicated to St Peter and one to St John Lateran. The former adjoined the site of the martyrdom of St Peter. It was 380 feet (116 m) long, and 212 feet (65 m) wide. The nave was 80 feet (24 m) wide and 100 feet (30 m) high. Its great size was worthy of its rank as the first church of Christendom, and the most impressive place of worship. St Paul beyond the Walls resembled St Peter's in its plan. Santa Maria Maggiore was smaller in size and had Ionic columns supporting architraves.

The basilica was the model for church architecture in Rome with very little change in plan until the Renaissance. The earlier examples, in the main, made use of Corinthian columns and capitals from old temples.

During the fifth and sixth centuries, Ravenna had a number of magnificent buildings constructed. It became the place where Early Christian and Byzantine traditions met, and basilican and circular plans were both made use of. There were two churches dedicated to St Apollinaris— S. Apollinare Nuovo A.D. 520, and S. Apollinare in Classe A.D. 538. Both had fine mosaics, and round brick bell towers adjoining them, which later became typical of north Italian churches. All the earlier churches were built facing the east.

The basilican type of church became usual in Italy, and many of them continued to have wooden roofs long after the emergence of the Gothic style.

The main departures from the early type were external, when the outside was decorated with marble or with successive arcades, until eventually clustered piers, pointed arches, vaulting etc. changed the basilican form gradually into what became known as the Romanesque and Gothic styles.

Christian architecture produced a number of outstanding structures in Syria. The most notable were those built by Constantine: the Church of the Nativity in Bethlehem, the Church of the Ascension at Jerusalem (a magnificent octagonal church on the site of Solomon's Temple) and a similar one at Antioch. They were very large and exceptionally magnificent.

It was not very long before Christian architecture in Syria broke away from the Roman tradition. Hard stone in plenty and a lack of clay or brick made an independent approach necessary which resulted in the development of changed types of architecture, the progress of which was halted by the Mohammedan conquest in the seventh century. Piers of masonry began to replace classical columns, and the ceilings in small churches were often made with stone slabs. At first the apse, which was sometimes square, was within the main rectangle of the plan. Turrets, gables and porches transformed the exterior. Vaulting was rare, but arches were used to good effect. Circular plans were often employed in Syria during the sixth century. Frequently the circle was within a square, leaving four niches at the corners of the square.

Such circles within squares might have been the prototypes of Byzantine churches such as St Sergius at Constantinople (Istanbul) and San Vitale at Ravenna.

Elsewhere in the Eastern world there were many early churches. Salonica, for example, had several basilicas and a number of dominical churches. At various places in Asia Minor, and in Egypt, Nubia and Algiers, there were examples of early churches and basilicas.

10
Byzantine

When Constantine chose Byzantium as the new capital of his empire, it was practically in ruins. He rebuilt it and renamed it Constantinople. He built a magnificent church, St Sophia's. The plan was square, but this was broken by a portico and two entrance courts. At the back was a rounded recess. Of the two courts the outer one was a square with arcades around it and a fountain in the centre. The Inner Court was for penitents. Within the interior the square of the plan was repeated; four huge piers were connected by four arches and carried the great dome. A number of small domes led up to this central dome. The basic difference between a Byzantine dome and a Roman one is that the former was carried over a square space and the latter over a round space. Roman domes were perfect hemispheres whereas Byzantine domes were slightly flattened.

The Byzantine method of colourful decoration was the use of mosaic, with scraps of marble and glass. St Sophia was very rich in its decor; its entire interior glittered and glimmered with many colours.

The artisans who rebuilt the city were Greeks from Asia Minor and the Aegean Islands, and Syrians, and their art strongly influenced the Byzantine. Trade with the East must have brought in some of the Oriental preference for brilliant colours and minute decoration. The methods of vaulting, which were more varied than the Roman, might also have been of Asiatic origin. They borrowed from the Romans their ideas of structural art, thus distributing the weights of vaulted structures on large and isolated support points with the strengthening by buttresses inside and outside. They also made use of the Roman monolithic columns of polished stone. Under these many influences the Byzantine architects worked out their own systems of construction and decoration, which gave their work a new and typical character of its own.

There is no clear dividing line between early Christian and Byzantine architecture. The former was represented mainly by the basilica with three or five aisles and wooden roofs. Only rarely did they make use of

The Sultan Ahmet mosque in Istanbul, Turkey.

the vault, and the dome, in the main, was used to cover small tombs and baptisteries. Nearly all the Byzantine structures were vaulted and/or domed. There is not a great deal of uniformity in the plans or in the forms of vaulting. The Byzantines substituted brick and stone masonry for concrete. They used stone alone or in combination with brick, and it was not uncommon for them to alternate the two materials course for course. When piers were intended to support really heavy loads, the stone was very carefully cut and fitted, and sometimes clamped with iron.

Byzantine art exercised a strong influence in Europe and in Asia. Constantinople's relations with Ravenna, Genoa and Venice resulted in the use of traditional Byzantine architecture in those places, when Byzantine builders copied some of the buildings and used some of their plans. St Mark's in Venice was originally copied from the Church of the Apostles at Constantinople, and San Lorenzo in Milan was Byzantine in plan and had an octagonal rotunda, four apses and a surrounding aisle.

The Byzantine style became the official style of the Greek Church in Russia, Greece and the Balkans. The Russians introduced bulbous domes. In Greece the churches tended to be small. The greatest and most numerous offsprings of Byzantine architecture came after Constantinople fell to the Turks in 1453, in their building of mosques.

11
Islamic

While the Empire of Byzantium still prospered, Islamic culture and religion was sweeping its way through Western Asia and across the Mediterranean. The architecture of conquered peoples such as the Copts, Syrians and Greeks was influenced and inspired by Muslim traditions, and the philosophy and poetry of the Islamic world brought about changes in their architecture, giving it distinctive qualities which were neither Christian nor Byzantine. There were developments not only in the shape but also in the decoration of the buildings. The Muhammadans had no great traditions of their own in art, and were readily influenced by the art of other civilizations, in the same way that their religion had adopted parts of other faiths. Delicate surface ornamentation became most important, although paintings and sculpture were noticeable by their absence. So an architectural form evolved which was unmistakably Islamic in character, and the mosques, palaces and tombs typified the culture.

The mosque was the focal point of the Muslim community—it provided many services other than a purely religious one. The only furniture was the pulpit, but the floors were covered in rugs and carpets on which the congregation knelt. The buildings were decorated with mosaics, ceramics, and relief carvings. These were not figurative designs, but elaborate calligraphic quotations from the Koran, with naturalistic and geometric designs. All mosques contain the mihrab, which indicates the direction of Mecca, towards which the faithful direct their prayers. Although the form and shape of mosques vary greatly, they all have a minaret or tower from which the priest (muezzin) calls the faithful to prayer. The earliest form was in open plan style.

The Great Mosque at Damascus (built A.D. 710–15) was built on such a plan. It was rectangular in shape, and at each corner was a minaret. Its present dome is of modern construction, but there is evidence that there was a much earlier dome. On three sides of the mosque were roofed arcades, and a prayer hall ran along the fourth side.

In Egypt, one of the first open plan mosques to be built (dated between

Dome of the Shah Nematolah mosque in Kerman, Iran.

45

A.D. 965 and 1171) was that of Al Hakim. The façade was beautifully decorated with carved geometric patterns and exquisite calligraphy. The largest open plan mosque in existence, however, is the Great Mosque of Samarra, which has an unusual winding minaret, nearly 90 feet (27 m) high, and is surrounded by a high wall, set with many towers.

In Persia, mosques with four open vaulted halls, or ivans, were preferred. One of the most magnificent mosques in Iran is the Great Mosque of Isfahan, constructed between A.D. 1072 and 1092. This beautiful building has a huge dome nearly 64 feet (20 m) in diameter over the mihrab chamber; opposite this at the northern end of the mosque is a smaller dome.

Domed mosques were generally rectangular in shape, the whole structure being drawn together under the central dome. They are largely associated with Turkey, though there are exceptions. Variations of the single-domed design sometimes appear, where a number of small domes could be used to cover the central area. One of the finest examples of a domed mosque in existence is that at Edirne, which was built between A.D. 1567 and 1575.

Palaces built to Islamic traditions are many and varied, according to their location and the time of their construction. At Samarra, near Baghdad, one of the earliest palaces was built. It was constructed of unbaked brick, however, and now no longer stands. It consisted of many rooms, including a throne room, and had grounds with a fountain. A stone palace built in the eighth century still survives at Ukhaydir. In Turkey, a large palace at the Topkapi Saray was begun in the fifteenth century and extensions and additional rooms built on right up to the nineteenth century. It has many pavilions, small palaces and other apartments, within extensive and beautiful gardens. One of the most exquisite and best-known Islamic palaces is that of the Alhambra in Spain, built during the fourteenth century by the rulers of Granada at that time, Yusef I and his son Muhammed V.

Within this brief glimpse of the vast world of Islamic architecture, we cannot fail to mention the superb palaces of the Moguls in India. The Red Forts at Delhi and at Agra are both masterpieces, stately and magnificent in a unique blend of red sandstone and white marble. They combined the very best architectural skills of Persia and India. At Fatehpur Sikri stands the superb palace which was built in 1569–72 by the great emperor Akbar, which surely is a tribute to the architectural styles of both the Hindu and Islamic traditions.

Finally, there are the tombs which perhaps are amongst the most

The Red Fort at Delhi.

impressive in the world. A typical layout of an Islamic tomb generally consisted of a chamber, over which a dome was erected. The shape of the dome and the detail of the lower chamber varied according to the date of the tomb and where it was built. Some of the finest Islamic tombs were those of the Samanids at Bukhara. Timur's tomb at Samarkand was particularly distinctive. It consisted of an octagonal base, set with a fluted blue dome. The interior was decorated with semi-precious stones, and geometric inscriptions adorned the exterior. The tomb was initially built for his nephew, but as he himself died before it had been completed, he was buried in it. The Gunbad-i Qabus, which was built near the shore of the Caspian Sea by the ruler of Gurgan in the eleventh century, had a tower and a pointed, tent-like roof. The mausoleum at Sultaniya had a large dome on an octagonal base with a minaret standing at the apex of each angle.

At Agra in India stands the legendary Taj Mahal. This tomb, constructed in white marble, combines the greatest traditions of Persia and India, using the skill, craftsmanship and artistry of the mason, the

47

jeweller and the calligrapher to the full. A beautiful marble lattice-work screen surrounds the imitation tombs of Shah Jehan and his wife, whereas the real tombs are stored in the vault below. The Taj, as one of the wonders of the world, can perhaps be regarded as the greatest testament to Islamic architecture.

12
Early Medieval—Romanesque
—Norman

In the years immediately after the fall of Rome and the partition of the Roman Empire, a new style of architecture began to develop, which was based on that of the early Christian builders, with modifications from the Roman and Byzantine. The Celtic and Germanic races were becoming Christian and were coming under the influence of the Christian Church. Romanesque architecture, which spread throughout the western part of the old Roman Empire, and also Poland and Scandinavia, was largely ecclesiastical. The requirements and discipline of the Church moulded this new style of the builder. Wherever the Roman Catholic Church was, the building was Romanesque. In those countries where the religion was Greek Orthodox, the building style was Byzantine.

Regional styles such as Lombard, Saxon, Norman, Carolingian and Rhenish can all be classed as Romanesque, and these prevailed for over 600 years until the development of Gothic architecture.

In the Middle Ages, Italy was placed halfway between the civilization of the Eastern Empire and the barbarism of the West. Architecture got its inspiration through cultural contacts and the influences of the church, but provincialism and the diversity of the various States assisted in resulting in variations in style: the Lombard, Tuscan-Romanesque, Italo-Byzantine, Siculo-Arabic and Basilican, which continued to be practised.

Lombard churches were often vaulted, although the plans were basilican. The naves were narrow, and instead of rows of columns a few large piers of masonry carried the pier arches and supported the ribs of the groined vaulting. The spaciousness and elegance of the basilicas gave way to a massive dignity. Sometimes the choir was raised above the nave to allow for a crypt and confessional below.

Outside, the Lombard style of church was relatively simple. The façades usually had a single broad gable, the three aisles being suggested by flat or round pilasters dividing the façade. Many churches had a bell tower or campanile adjoining them.

The campaniles of Italy were usually separate structures, square in plan. Two early ones adjoined the churches of S. Apollinare at Ravenna. They were built in the sixth century A.D. and were circular in shape, with very few openings, although the upper storey had large arch openings to allow the sound of the bells to escape. By the ninth century A.D., campaniles were a regular feature in Rome. The Roman ones were square and had little decoration; they had few openings below the upper storey, where arched windows beneath a pyramid-shaped roof let out the sound of the bells.

In various Italian cities campaniles varied in design and in the material of their construction. In Lombardy the towers were of red brick construction and the plans were often octagonal. One of the finest was that of S. Gottardo at Milan, and there were typical examples at Verona, Padua and many other cities.

The most famous Italian campaniles were those of Florence, Pisa and Venice. That adjoining the Duomo at Florence was considered to be one of the most beautiful. The Leaning Tower of Pisa, dated A.D. 1174, was of unique plan. Externally, it consisted of arcades on top of each other. The Campanile of St Mark's in Venice, begun in A.D. 874 and ultimately completed in the sixteenth century, was about 325 feet (99 m) high. It was rebuilt to the original design in 1902.

The Tuscan Romanesque was a more elegant design than the Lombard Basilicas in plan; it had column arcades and timber ceilings. Externally, the use of white or coloured bands or panelled veneers of marble suggested Byzantine influence. Sometimes they had external wall arcades which stood the full height of the wall. The Duomo of Pisa, built A.D. 1063–1118, was typical of this style. It measured 312 feet by 118 feet (95 m × 36 m) and had five aisles and an elliptical dome which was constructed later. Its font was richly arcaded. The circular baptistery, A.D. 1153, and the Leaning Tower of Pisa with the Duomo formed the most remarkable group of ecclesiastical buildings in Italy.

The Church of S. Miniato near Florence, built A.D. 1013–60, was a basilica in plan but had a nave divided into three by two transverse arches which supported a painted timber roof. The interior was magnificent in black and white marble, and the exterior had wall arches and veneered panels of black and white marble.

In many parts of east and south Italy, Lombard and Byzantine styles mingled, and in Sicily the Byzantine influence showed itself in domes and other details.

In Western Europe unrest and disorder held back any architectural progress, and it was not until the eleventh century A.D. that there was

Medieval castle of Kolossi, near Limassol, Cyprus.

any real building activity, and this was largely due to the monasteries which stood alone as centres of culture and order. They were rich in men and in land and they explored new ways to meet their own architectural needs. They had little technical training, but as they gained in experience they gained in skill, and in mastery of construction. Gradually they developed in taste and elegance of design.

At the same time, military architecture developed and Europe became dotted with imposing castles which combined strength and artistry with the usefulness of these buildings in times of war.

The Romanesque architecture of the eleventh and twelfth centuries A.D. although not entirely ecclesiastic was predominantly so. Although there were local variations by reason of their character and purpose, there was a certain degree of uniformity. Generally speaking, the monastic builders attempted to adapt the plan of the basilica to the requirements of vaulted construction. Enormous walls, round arches, richly carved mouldings, clustered piers, with capitals imitating the Corinthian, were all common to the Romanesque architecture of France, Germany, England and Spain.

In France, however, which was a group of feudal provinces with little allegiance to the King in Paris, architecture varied considerably from region to region and displayed the many influences to which each was subjected. The south was Gallic and Roman; the north and east were influenced by Teutons, Goths, Burgundians, Franks and Normans. Provence maintained close relations with Venice and the East and was greatly influenced by its classical remains and traditions. Their churches were nearly all barrel vaulted, and they showed Byzantine and Lombard influence in their sculpture and decoration. Domed churches in obvious imitation of Byzantine also appeared in Aquitaine, and there were instances of the substitution of the Latin cross for the Greek in the plan which indicated the tendency to work out new ideas or develop old ones.

The Duchy of Burgundy, which defied the King for centuries, had monastic centres which were mothers of their own orders, and their influences were very extensive. Cluny was the mother house of the Clunisians who were foremost in architectural development. They built a huge monastery in A.D. 1089 and also an abbey at Vézelay. Cîteaux was the mother house of the Cistercians, who largely insisted on architectural simplicity, and they replaced the apse and ambulatory with a square east end in their churches. This had a great influence on later English architecture.

There was not a great deal of architectural activity in the King's own territory until the middle of the twelfth century A.D., about the beginning of the Gothic period, although in Normandy at Caen some outstanding churches were constructed between A.D. 1046 and 1120 which had a high clerestory achieved by six-part vaulting. This expedient appeared in early Gothic churches in both France and Great Britain.

French Romanesque architecture varied with the local influences, but, except in Aquitaine, most churches had round arches. Walls were of rubble faced with stones; windows and doors were wide in order to reduce the obstruction of the size of the walls. Sculptured figures were used more in the south than in the north, and interior piers were cylindrical and often clustered. Each shaft bore an independent capital which had some resemblance to the Corinthian.

Externally the churches were flat and plain. They had simple mouldings and the early towers were not often joined to the body of the church. The western porches were very imposing with their huge arches, carved mouldings and clustered piers.

Usually grouped around the abbey churches of this time were a number of buildings which consisted of kitchens, stores, refectories, chapter halls, cells and cloisters, the last usually being of remarkable beauty.

The development of architecture was slower in Germany than it was in France. In its vast territory there was no real unity. The earliest churches were constructed with timber, and the use of stone instead of wood made progress very slow. Buildings showing Byzantine and classical influences were erected during the period A.D. 800–919. These included the palatine chapel of Charlemagne at Aix-la-Chapelle. It was an octagonal domed structure surrounded by a vaulted aisle. Its porch had turrets on either side. A basilica with transepts and a choir at each end was built in A.D. 803 in the great monastery at Fulda. The choirs were above the level of the nave and had crypts beneath them.

The early churches in Saxony were basilican in plan and were without vaulting, except perhaps in the crypts. Often the huge piers with which they were built were clustered, and were rectangular and alternated. Sometimes short columns were used either alone or alternating with piers. Externally two, four or six towers, either square or circular, often gave a more interesting aspect to otherwise plain structures.

The Lombard influence was frequently discernible in the exteriors of a number of Rhenish churches, not only because of their size but also because of their plan and the picturesque exteriors. The massing of turrets large and small with the lofty roof of the nave and with the apses, and the arcading on the outside walls gave to these churches an exceptional beauty. This method of exterior design probably came from the Lombard churches of Northern Italy.

Of secular architecture in Germany during this period there was little other than the great feudal castles which were more works of military engineering than of architecture. The palace of Charlemagne at Aix was a vast group of buildings which were constructed partly of marble. The Kaiserburg at Goslar had an imposing assembly hall with two aisles and arched windows. At Brunswick the residence of Henry the Lion had a chapel and great hall and two fortified towers.

Prior to the Norman Conquest there was very little architecture in the British Isles. Saxon architecture was primitive, and indicated limited resources and little skill. It had also suffered from the incursions of the

Saxon church at Kilpeck, Herefordshire.

Danes and Norsemen. With the coming of the Normans there was great activity in building churches. William the Conqueror founded a number, and there was an endeavour for them to outdo the abbeys and churches built in Normandy. There were some differences—those built in Britain were longer, narrower and not so high as those built in France. The cathedrals of Durham and Norwich were built at about this time.

The Anglo-Norman builders used the same general features as the

Romanesque builders of Normandy. Their structures were more picturesque, less elegant and less refined. Corinthian capitals were rare,
however, and simpler forms were used. Nevertheless both styles had
much in common; heavy walls, recessed arches and clustered piers were
typical of the architectural structures of both Normandy and Britain.

The interiors of the larger churches were very similar to the French
Norman structures of the same time. Many of the abbeys and cathedrals
had wooden ceilings. The piers were often round, as at Gloucester, Hereford, Southwell and Bristol Cathedrals and also Tewkesbury Abbey. At
Durham and Waltham, clustered piers alternating with round ones were
used, whereas at Peterborough, Norwich and Winchester clustered
piers alone were used in the transepts.

The façades were simple, but the doorways were adorned with carved
mouldings and clustered jamb-shafts. The zigzag was often employed,
and also birds' heads with the beaks pointing towards the centre of the
arch. In the larger churches the doorways appeared to be insignificantly
small, but they were better proportioned to the façades of the smaller
churches. The round arch was replaced by the pointed arch in the latter
part of the twelfth century.

When Toledo was captured from the Moors in 1062, this was the
beginning of the end of Muslim rule in Spain. A number of churches
were built in the north, and all of them clearly showed French-Roman-
esque influence. There were, of course, modifications; long naves and
transepts and short choirs were common to them all. The dome of the
Panteon of S. Isidoro at Leon, and that over the choir in old Salamanca
Cathedral, were probably derived from the domes of Aquitaine and
Anjou. Nearly all these churches had groined vaulting over the aisles,
and barrel vaults over the nave, as in Auvergne and Burgundy.

The Spanish churches were not so very different from their French
contemporaries and, as in England and in France, the doorways were
the most ornate part of the work, with rich carving and sculpture. Perhaps there was greater variety in the style of the façades.

Although there were numerous examples of Islamic architecture, they
had little influence over the architecture of this time, largely, perhaps,
because of the hatred the Christians had for the Muslims and everything
to do with them.

13
Gothic

In Western Europe, from about 1150 to about 1500, there developed a style of architecture known as the Gothic. It grew in fact out of the Romanesque, in England, France, Germany, Spain, the Low Countries and Switzerland, and spread to Hungary, Portugal and Poland. It tackled the same problems, and its basic principles were the same. The outstanding feature of Gothic architecture was the pointed arch.

The twelfth century brought many economic, social and political changes which marked it and the subsequent century as outstanding in the history of the progress of mankind. There was a mighty struggle for supremacy between the Crown, the barons, the Pope and the bishops; and the Church began to emerge as a power behind and above all else, as also did the State, so that there were in fact two powerful bodies divinely appointed to govern the lives of men.

Ecclesiastical architecture developed rapidly, with the growth in power of the Church, which was not slow to make full use of the guilds of masons and builders and their constantly growing skills and experience.

Gothic architecture changed as the craftsmen acquired more skill and experience. It applied two principles which had been recognized by the Romans and Byzantines and later revived by the Romanesque builders.

By substituting groined vaults for barrel vaults it made it possible to concentrate strains on isolated supports. Masses of masonry were concentrated on these points as if on legs. Walls became the filling between piers or buttresses, and in time large expanses of stained glass windows filled the spaces. At Sainte Chapelle in Paris, which was built 1242–47, groined vaults were based on slender shafts supported by deep external buttresses. The spaces between them were filled entirely by stained glass windows and stone tracery. The cathedrals of Gerona (Spain) and of Alby (France) utilized the same idea, but in these instances the buttresses were internal and were used to separate the various chapels.

In Roman architecture, the vaulting was resisted by the mass of surroundings, but, in Gothic, flying half-arches to external buttresses transmitted the pressure. The flying buttress reached the peak of its development in the cathedrals of northern and central France in the thirteenth and fourteenth centuries. External buttresses which had been decorated with small gables were later capped with pinnacles rather like tiny steeples.

Transmitted thrusts and concentration of strains led to ribbed vaulting and the pointed arch. Ribbed vaulting resulted from difficulties experienced in the building of large groined vaults. Groined vaults were built as one structure on wooden centerings. The Romanesque builders built a skeleton of ribs, two wall ribs, two transverse ribs and two groin ribs which intersected at the centre of the vault, which was thus divided into four triangular portions supported by the groin ribs. The Gothic builders made the ribs elaborately decorative as well as scientifically useful.

When oblong vaults were constructed and a narrow vault intersected a wide one, difficulties were created which were overcome by the introduction of the pointed arch, which made it possible for a narrow vault

The 'great cloisters' of Fountains Abbey, Ripon, Yorkshire.

to be made as high as a wide one. Groin ribs were, in the main, round; but the transverse ribs and the wall ribs were always pointed arches, which were in effect the most convenient shape for these ribs. The pointed arch was used in the shape of the windows and pier arches. The inner stone roof could not be entirely weatherproof because of the vaulting which made a number of protrusions and exterior pockets which would hold rain, ice and snow. So it was necessary for a protective outer wooden roof itself covered by tile, slate, copper or lead to be built over the stone vaulting. The growth in size of windows, and reduction of the size of the actual walls automatically resulted in the use of more stained glass. This tended to develop the use of stone tracery, which was most necessary to support the glass. Originally it consisted of decorative openings in circles and quatrefoils as if pierced through stone slabs, filling the space over coupled pointed arch windows. As time went on the form of the stonework became lighter and richly shaped. The circular and geometric designs gave way to more flowing tracery or, as in England, rectangles. The character of the stone tracery employed often identified the period and style of Gothic architecture.

During the period 1200–1500, the changes in construction gave rise to modifications in the established basilica plan; changed conditions and ecclesiastical requirements also resulted in modifications. Gothic church architecture largely consisted of cathedrals which differed in many ways from the monastic churches. The choirs of cathedrals were greatly lengthened and the transepts were made shorter. Choirs had two and sometimes four aisles which were often carried round the apse end. The spaces between the buttresses were filled in with chapels. In England the choir often had a square end in the east, and often, too, there were secondary transepts which together with the greater length and narrowness of the plan gave the English cathedrals a character of their own.

With these general modifications of the basilica plan, there was a tendency towards an increase in height and in slenderness of various parts of the structure. The clerestory became more lofty; the arcaded gallery beneath it, the pointed arches on the high piers, the numerous slender clustered shafts and the slimming down of the piers gave the interiors of Gothic churches an entirely different aspect from those of the Romanesque buildings, which were more massive, simpler and lower in construction.

Externally, the addition of towers and spires made a complete transformation. The pinnacles on top of the buttresses, the stone tracery on the windows and the sculptured portals all combined to produce effects of great beauty in marked contrast to the simple Romanesque exteriors.

The builders who sculptured the capitals and other adornments of the early Gothic cathedrals followed the tendency of the later monastic builders to look to nature for suggestions of form. During the thirteenth century the sculptors freely adapted vigorous plant life to their carvings in stone. Later, cleverness and imitation took the place of invention and the slender carving went into minute detail, with a great deal of decoration on every available surface. During the fifteenth century there was a tendency for much of the carving to be too small and lacking in vigour. The builders seemed to devote themselves to concentrating on elaborating the decorative detail after having worked their structural ideas to their perfect conclusion.

Military architecture, which had been developed under the feudal system, was at its peak in the thirteenth and fourteenth centuries. During the fifteenth century, however, the growth of organized national governments and the introduction of the use of artillery in war changed the old ideas of defensive building. Hitherto a castle had been in effect a fortified place to house the lord and his retainers. Now it had two functions, as a palace and a fort, and usually there was a city wall with curtain walls and towers as an outer defence for the whole town. However, generally speaking, Gothic architecture triumphed in its construction of cathedrals and large churches, and it was in fact the requirements of these buildings which gave Gothic architecture its beautiful form and character.

In France, the church builders led those of other countries in inventiveness, quickness and directness of achievement, and in their overall artistry. The great period of cathedral building in France was in the latter half of the twelfth century and the first half of the thirteenth. The bishops supported the King and the church rapidly recovered its old power and influence. Cathedrals which were in effect the throne churches of the bishops were popular among the people. New cathedrals were built in many places in Normandy, Burgundy and Champagne and these new constructions were warmly supported by the people in protest against the excesses of feudalism. Much building was made immediately necessary, also, by the need to replace structures which had collapsed because of the faulty Romanesque vaulting, or which had been destroyed by fire. Many cathedrals were reconstructed during the period 1130 to 1200, and a large number of new ones were begun. After 1250 the activity slackened off and only a few more cathedrals were started; and French architecture concerned itself more with completing and remodelling existing cathedrals than with building new ones.

Perhaps the biggest change from the basilican basic plan was the ambulatory, which was formed by continuing the aisles round the apse and adding chapels between the apse buttresses. These chapels replaced the earlier chapels of earlier churches and added to the interior beauty. At Notre Dame in Paris there was at first a double ambulatory, and the chapels were added at a later date. Chartres and Le Mans had double ambulatories, but after 1220 only single ones appeared. Often the Lady Chapel was longer than other chapels, as at Le Mans, Rouen and Bayeux. Most cathedrals had chapels on the sides of the choir, whereas Notre Dame amongst others had chapels at the sides of the nave.

Bourges Cathedral, which was begun in 1190, resembled closely Notre Dame in plan, as both were intended to accommodate large numbers of people in their very broad central aisles and double aisles at the sides. Bourges, however, had no side aisle galleries and its vaulting, although later, was inferior to that of Notre Dame. Both had six-part vaults above the nave.

Noyon, Soissons and Senli, although built about the same time as Notre Dame, were far less completely Gothic; in contrast, the groined vaulting of the cathedral at Le Mans was very heavy and primitive, although it also had been built about the same time as Notre Dame.

In the south and west of France the builders were largely influenced by the Aquitainian styles, and stuck to the square plan and dome-shaped vaulting bay. They used groin ribs in imitation of the north, but their vaults were still built like domes and the groin ribs had no real function. However, in about 1145–60 the cathedral of St Maurice at Angers was given square groin-ribbed vaults, domed in shape, but not in construction. This idea became generally adopted in the west and was later followed by English architects.

The church architects of Northern France discontinued using the square vaulting bays and six-part vaults early in the thirteenth century, and adopted groin ribs and the pointed arch which simplified their building of vaults in oblong bays. Each bay of the nave had its own complete vault. Perhaps the earliest example of this system was the cathedral at Chartres which was begun in about 1194. Practically all the large churches begun after 1200 had the fully developed oblong vault.

As the height of clerestorys increased, the use of double aisles made it necessary to pay special attention to the buttresses. The choirs of Chartres, Notre Dame, Bourges, Rouen and Rheims were examples of

1 Part of the palace at Knossos in Crete. Dating from the pre-Hellenic period,
much of the palace was destroyed by a natural disaster *c.* 1400 B.C.

2 The famous Lion Gate at Mycenae. This is an early example of the use of stone decorative sculpture in architecture.

3   The huge obelisk of Hatshepsut at Karnak in Egypt is 97 ft (30 m) in height.
Obelisks are a particular feature in Egyptian architecture and are thought to have
been symbolic of the sun.

4 The entrance to the great temple of Amen-Ra at Karnak, built *c.* 1570–1085 B.C. is flanked by sculptured rams.

5 Doric columns at Olympia, Greece. The Doric order culminated in the magnificent architecture of the Parthenon at Athens.

6 One of the best preserved Greek theatres is at Delphi, famous for the Oracle.
Built *c.* 160 B.C., it had a tiered system of seating.

7 Set on a hill, much still remains of the Doric temple of Aphaea at Aegina.

8 Dodoni was the site of the earliest Greek oracles and was dedicated to Zeus.

9 One of the most famous Roman sites in Britain is that of *Aquae Sulis*, present-day Bath, where the Roman baths can still be seen.

10   The Arch of Constantine, near the Colosseum in Rome, was built in A.D. 315 to
celebrate the Emperor's victory over Maxentius.

11   The city of Pompeii was destroyed by volcanic lava from Vesuvius in A.D. 79.
     Many of the buildings were preserved under the ash.

12   Makri, in Greece. Many small communities in rural Greece have had the same
     lifestyle for hundreds of years.

13 The Fire Temple at Persepolis, the city built during the reign of the great Persian
ruler, Darius I. Much of the original building still remains.

14 The stupendous Kailasa temple is carved out of black volcanic rock. A great Hindu achievement, it is one of a group of temples at Ellora in India.

15 The great mosques of Iran, such as this one in Isfahan, are famous for the artistry
and craftsmanship of their tiled domes.

16 Interior of a mosque, again at Isfahan. There is an absence of adornment on the walls apart from geometric and calligraphic designs.

17 Built in the form of a vast Chariot of the Sun, the Temple of the Sun at Konarak, India, is an awesome achievement.

18 The watchtower in the courtyard of the Muhammad Ali mosque in Egypt.

19 The Pavilion at the Agra Fort, India, was built in imitation of the primitive Bengali fisherman's hut.

20 Ceramic tilework of outstanding quality in the Gulestan Palace, Tehran.

21 The Taj Mahal at Agra, in India, was built in 1635, as a mausoleum for the wife of the Emperor Shah Jehan.

22   A Jain victory tower at Chittore in Rajasthan, India. This is a fine example of
Jain architecture displaying the superimposition of different planes.

23 Detail of the exquisite ceramic decoration of the Kadimyah mosque in Baghdad, Iraq.

24   The courtyard and tower of La Mezquita in Cordoba, Spain.

25 The door of Al-Hakan at La Mezquita in Cordoba, showing typical Moorish influence.

26 The well-known Lion Court of the Alhambra Palace in Granada, Spain, is a superb example of Moorish architecture. The delicate tracery of its arches is noteworthy.

27 S. Sophia, typifying the splendour of Byzantine architecture, was built as a Christian church but converted into a mosque when the Turks captured Constantinople.

28 The Byzantine Empire once controlled the whole Mediterranean area. Its immense influence can be seen in this building in Ligourio, Greece.

29 The island of Malta encompasses many different architectural periods. This corner of Mdina dates to late medieval times.

30 The façade of the Corn Market in Mantua, Italy. The Renaissance encouraged the construction of fine buildings not only for ecclesiastic and domestic purposes but also for commerce.

31 Norwich Cathedral was completed in the twelfth century. In the late fifteenth century the original spire, which had been struck by lightning, was replaced by the present one.

32 Notre Dame, Paris, is one of the most loved cathedrals in Europe. Of early Gothic
style, it commands a prominent position in the heart of the city. Its rose windows
are renowned.

33 Ruins of a Norman house in Christchurch, Dorset. The Priory may be seen in the background.

34 Ferrara, in Italy, was ruled by the d'Este family during the Renaissance. From their castle they dominated the life and culture of the city.

35 The dome of Florence Cathedral. Designed by the great Renaissance architect, Brunelleschi, it was built in 1436, and the lantern added two years later.

36   The simple, functional lines of the buildings on this Japanese farm are a feature of oriental traditions in architecture.

37   The Forbidden City of Peking, in China. The pagoda-style roof is a particular characteristic of Chinese architecture.

38 Interior view of the dome of St Peter's Basilica, Rome. Mosaics of the four
evangelists appear around the lower part of the dome.

39 The Russian Orthodox Church in Florence. The arrangement of five elegant domes each surmounted by a cross are characteristic of Russian churches.

40 'Scottish' houses in Veere, Holland. Gabled façades were a popular feature of Dutch architecture in the late sixteenth and early seventeenth centuries.

41 Y Plâs in Llangollen, Wales, shows the traditional 'black and white' architecture
of the Tudor period.

42 Many English architects of the Elizabethan era were influenced by Flemish thought.
This house is at Varwerkbouw, Gulpen, in Holland.

43 Beams for Tudor houses such as this one at Lower Brockhampton, Herefordshire, could not be planed to exact specifications—hence the rather 'wavy' appearance.

THE : FEAR : OF : THE : LORD : IS : A : FOUNTAIN : OF : LIFE :

44 Chester is noted for its seventeenth-century timber-framed houses, built by the merchant classes when the city was a flourishing centre of trade and commerce.

45 Typical façades of houses facing the famous canals of Amsterdam. Many of the
    houses are extremely narrow and are topped by traditional gabled roofs.

46 Azay-Le-Rideau, a magnificent Renaissance château in the Loire valley, France.

47   Part of the old city of Bruges in Belgium. Once a prosperous wool-making centre, the city retains much of its medieval appearance.

48 The splendid baroque and rococo façades of the buildings in the Grand-Place, Brussels, were built during the late seventeenth and early eighteenth centuries.

49 The façade of this beautiful building in Poland demonstrates the delicate architectural style of the Polish people. Note the fine sculptured figures at the top of
the building.

50 Blenheim Palace, presented to the Duke of Marlborough in recognition of his victories, and designed by the great English architect, Sir John Vanbrugh, in 1705, may be considered the culmination of English baroque architecture.

51 St Paul's Cathedral in London, was designed by Sir Christopher Wren in 1675 and was completed thirty-five years later. Inside the dome is the famous 'Whispering Gallery'.

52 Carlton Terrace, in London. Neo-classical in style, it was one of a number of buildings designed for George IV by John Nash.

53 Charlotte Square, Edinburgh. These impressive Georgian buildings were planned by the famous Robert Adam.

54   The city of Dublin is renowned for its well-proportioned and elegant Georgian architecture.

55   The Georgian houses of Regent's Park, London display the fine neo-classical motifs and mouldings popular in the early nineteenth century.

56 The Town Hall in the market square of Kuopio in Finland. Architectural traditions are very important in Finland, but many early timber buildings no longer stand.

57 Many homes in the U.S.A., particularly in New England, are of clap- or weather-boarded construction. This is the Ford Museum in Detroit, Michigan.

58 The well-known Manhattan skyline of New York. In the centre of this view of the skyscrapers the Empire State Building can be seen.

59 Government House, Hong Kong. The architecture of the twentieth century saw a move towards a more streamlined approach.

60 The London Telecom Tower (formerly the Post Office Tower). Built in the mid-1960s, it was then the tallest building in Britain. Primarily functional, it also has a revolving restaurant for the public.

61 Coventry Cathedral, designed by Sir Basil Spence, was built to replace the old
cathedral which was badly damaged during World War 2.

62 The new city of Brasilia is a major example of twentieth-century city planning.
This photograph shows the cathedral.

63 The Opera House holds a prominent position in Sydney Harbour, Australia. When first planned, the 'shells' caused some controversy.

64 The Pompidou Centre in Paris. Known colloquially as 'Beaubourg', this building is unusual in that all the service piping has been constructed on the outside, making maximum use of the interior space.

the early use of flying buttresses. At first they were simple and not very high single half-arches across the side aisles, but at Notre Dame they traversed the double aisles in one leap. Buttresses and pinnacles were built over intermediate piers where they were double aisles beside the nave and choir, and the single flying arch was thus divided into two.

The Sainte Chapelle, built in Paris in 1242–47, exemplified Gothic design by its windows which measured 15 feet (4.6 m) by 50 feet (15 m). They occupied the entire wall space, and each was divided into four under the tracery of the windowhead. From each came a glow of colour from the stained glass. Other chapels of the same type were those in the palace at St Germain-en-Laye and in the chateau of Vincennes.

French cathedrals were nearly all of impressive size. That at Noyon, one of the smallest, was 333 feet (102 m) long. Sens was 354 feet (108 m); those at Laon, Bourges, Troyes, Notre Dame, Le Mans, Rouen and Chartres were from 396 to 437 feet (121–33 m) in length. Notre Dame measured 124 feet (38 m) across the five aisles of the nave, and Bourges was even wider. The span from the centres of the piers on either side of the centre aisles of these two cathedrals was 40 feet (12 m). The ridge of the vaulting of Notre Dame was 108 feet (33 m) above the pavement, Bourges 125 feet (38 m), Amiens 140 feet (43 m), and Beauvais 152 feet (46 m). The five aisles of the nave at Notre Dame were 124 feet (38 m) wide. Bourges was even wider.

An effect which dwarfed the width of the centre aisles in French cathedrals was the height of the vaulting, which was three to three-and-a-half times the width of the nave.

The porches were very striking features of most French churches. Romanesque porches were usually only as deep as the thickness of the front wall. Gothic builders, however, made them deeper by projecting the portals beyond the wall and topping them with very elaborate gables. The porches at Laon, Bourges, Amiens and Rheims were richly majestic and deep. The portals of the fifteenth and early sixteenth centuries were richly decorated in tracery, as at Abbeville, Alençon, and St Maclou at Rouen.

Vertical elements reached their fullest expression in the towers and belfries of churches. Lofty belfry roofs soon developed into spires up to 300 feet (91 m) or more high. Corner pinnacles and dormers assisted in developing square towers into octagonal pyramids. From 1200 the tendency was for design to be richer and the detail to become more complicated. Central spires were common in Normandy. French towers generally had lower storeys without openings, strong buttresses and large windows on the aisles of the belfry to let out the sound of the bells.

In the thirteenth and fourteenth centuries, French Gothic architecture was outstanding in its sculpture, particularly in its figures. There was great beauty in the doorways of the west portals of the cathedrals and among the multitudes of angels which beautified the arches. The niches in which these figures were set played a very important part in the exterior decoration of churches, as they were carved with great delicacy and skill. Small ornamental carving often took the form of foliage, but grotesque figures were frequently used, as in the case of gargoyles which discharged roof water clear of the building. Flowers and foliage were often employed in the decoration of capitals, corbels and finials, and in the twelfth and thirteenth centuries they were simple and vigorous and the capitals were taller and slender. After the middle of the thirteenth century, the carving was more real, the leaves larger and more mature, and the carving gave the impression of having been applied to the stone capital or moulding and no longer looked as if it had grown out of it. The detail and workmanship were finer and more in keeping with the lighter and more slender style of architecture. Tracery began to be used increasingly. It was employed more and more for its decorative properties and often when it had no real use in the structure.

Many cathedrals begun in the second half of the thirteenth century were completed only after a long delay; some were never really completed. In the case of Beauvais Cathedral, which was started in 1247, the choir and chapels were completed in 1270. Its central tower and lofty vaulting collapsed in 1284 and had to be rebuilt, with twice the number of piers and a reduced arch span. The central aisle was 51 feet (15 m) from the centres of the piers on each side and the top of the vault was 152 feet (46 m) high. Transepts were not added until after 1500. Cathedrals at Limoges and Narbonne begun in 1272 were never completed, and those at Meaux, Rodez, Toulouse and Alby, all begun in the thirteenth century, were not finished until the sixteenth century. During the period 1260 to 1350 much work was done on many incomplete cathedrals.

Around this time the wheel tracery of rose windows and the use of circular forms were very popular. The rose windows of Notre Dame (dated about 1257) were typical, as are those of Rouen Cathedral which were of a later date than Notre Dame. The façade of Amiens cathedral (dated about 1288) was also a fine example.

From the geometric tracery and profusion of decoration of this period there gradually evolved a style of intricate decoration which became known as the Flamboyant style, and this predominated until about 1525, the beginning of the Renaissance in France. Detail became rich and unusually elaborate. Slenderness of supports was carried to extremes and the openwork was like lace in its delicacy. Not all structures of this period were noted for the richness of their ornamentation; there were some like St Merri and St Séverin in Paris which were relatively bare and poor in design.

French architecture during the Gothic period was not confined entirely to cathedrals, and there was some monastic building. Many abbeys rebuilt their churches in the Gothic style or extended or remodelled existing buildings. Cloisters were erected and many new refectories and chapels were built with the cathedrals.

Some hospitals, like St Jean at Angers or those at Beaune, Chartres and Tonnerre, demonstrated the skill of the French architects in adapting their architecture to civil requirements. The Palais de Justice at Rouen was built between 1499 and 1508. In most of these examples of adaptation for civil purposes, wooden ceilings and roofs replaced those of stone if a greater span or economy was required. Wall spaces were not suppressed by the use of stained glass and tracery.

Houses, barns, granaries etc. were also designed on the same principles. An arch was used as a shop opening onto the street; two or three storeys might be lighted by clustered pointed arch windows. The front was gabled and the roof steep. Half timbered construction which enabled the upper storeys to project over the street began to supersede stone in the construction of town houses in the fourteenth and fifteenth centuries. Many such houses were elaborately designed. The oak uprights were carved and the stone filling between beams was often covered with coloured tiles.

The large houses or palaces of the nobles, archbishops and wealthy citizens often rivalled or even surpassed monastic buildings in their richness and splendour. The increasing power of the King and more settled conditions resulted in the construction of residences in the larger cities for the nobles, which were more comfortable than their fortified feudal castles. These palaces had large halls, staircases and courts; they were exceedingly picturesque with square or circular towers, slender turrets and elaborately carved detail.

Gothic architecture in Great Britain was slower in development but more uniform than that of France. It was less bold and majestic, but rich in its internal decoration. It was not, as in France, mainly an architecture of cathedrals; fewer new cathedrals were built, although the rebuilding of existing ones went on well into the fifteenth century. It developed in England under a strongly established royal power. With the suppression of the monasteries by Henry VIII, the monastic cathedrals were carried on by non-monastic clergy. Other cathedrals already run by non-monastic clergy were not interfered with in any way.

The pointed arch and ribbed vault were imported from France. Early examples were in the abbeys of Furness and Kirkstall and in the Temple Church, London, which was built in 1185.

The Norman choir at Canterbury, which was destroyed by fire in 1170, was rebuilt by William of Sens. The plan of the rebuilt choir closely resembled that of the cathedral at Sens. Its coupled round piers, capitals, pointed arches and vaulting were all of French style. These Gothic details slowly supplanted the use of the round arch and other typical Norman features hitherto prevailing, and for a period of half a century there was a mixture of both styles in many buildings. Lincoln Cathedral which was rebuilt in about 1192–1200 did not, however, have anything of the round arch style. Salisbury Cathedral, which was built between 1220 and 1258, was the first church in England to be built entirely in the new Gothic style. Extreme length, as in Norwich and Durham cathedrals, still persisted, and Salisbury was 480 feet (146 m) long. The simple four-part vault was typically French, but the double transepts, the square east end and the long choir were early English Gothic. Westminster Abbey, built 1245–69, showed much of the French influence with its external flying buttresses and internal height of 100 feet (30 m).

Many of the cathedrals in England underwent repeated remodellings over the years. Durham, Norwich and Oxford were Norman, but all had Gothic vaults. Ely, Rochester, Gloucester and Hereford had Norman naves and Gothic choirs. Winchester's Norman nave was remodelled and its choir was Early Gothic. Purely Gothic churches and cathedrals, except parish churches, were far less numerous in England than in France.

The Gothic style in England may be broadly divided into three main periods. The *Early English Period* (from 1175 to 1260) was simple, had dignity, and was pure in design. The *Decorated* or *Geometric Period* which extended from 1260 to about 1360 was light in construction and had great richness of decoration. The *Perpendicular Period* lasted from about 1360 until the sixteenth century, when the late introduction of Renaissance forms put an end to the Gothic style in England.

In England there was little change in the plans of churches. Gothic cathedrals and abbeys were like the Norman, long and very narrow, and the choirs were often nearly as long as the nave, and were almost invariably square at the east end. Canterbury and Westminster were exceptions and showed clear signs of the French influence. Secondary transepts occur frequently in English plans. Canterbury, Durham, Salisbury, Lincoln, Worcester, Wells and Hereford are examples. English cathedral plans also retained or included, from time to time, cloisters, libraries and halls, and grouped chapter houses and Lady Chapels with the main building. This was in marked contrast to those on the Continent.

The greatest of the French cathedrals—Amiens—was 478 feet (146 m) in length, whereas Ely was 565 feet (172 m). Amiens was, however, 140 feet (43 m) high and Ely only 75 feet (23 m). Notre Dame in Paris was 148 feet (45 m) wide, and those in England were usually only about 80 feet (24 m) or less.

The English Gothic design strenuously avoided being venturesome. Everything was kept moderate and anything extreme was avoided. This led to some gain in freedom of design and less obtrusion of structural elements externally. Where the clerestory was low, the flying buttress became less important as a feature. In many cases flying arches were hidden under the roofs of the aisles.

There was much richness and variety in English vaulting compared to the uniformity of the French, although a few of the early ones were very much like the French. Generally speaking, however, the English did not like, and tended to avoid, the twisted dome surfaces of the French vaults. They preferred horizontal ridges and straight courses in zigzag lines meeting at the ridge. The idea of ribbed construction took hold; when a large number of ribs were sprung from each point of support, the vaulting surfaces were divided into long narrow triangles which could easily be filled. The ridge was given a straight rib and decorated with rosettes and a vaulting rib at each intersection. The naves and choirs at Lincoln, Lichfield, Exeter and Westminster illustrated this. Later, minor ribs were introduced which connected the main ribs and formed complex star patterns. Vaults of this type were among the most beautiful to be found in England. The choir at Gloucester, 1337–77, was one of the richest. The naves of Tewkesbury Abbey, and of Canterbury and Winchester Cathedrals, built between 1360 and 1400, were all examples of this system, which are called star vaults. This type was also to be seen in Norwich Cathedral, the church at Sherborne, Dorset, and St George's Chapel at Windsor.

A further development could be seen in the vaults of Oxford Cathedral and the cloisters of Gloucester, when the diverging ribs were given a uniform curvature. This sort of vaulting was elaborately developed in the choir of King's College Chapel at Cambridge, and the Chapel of Henry VII at Westminster. These became known as fan vaults, and, although they were rich and sumptuous in appearance, they were not as satisfactory as the earlier ribbed vaults.

Perhaps the ribbed vaulting in the cathedral chapters at Lincoln, Westminster and Salisbury was the most beautiful; the ribs radiated from the central column to the sides and points of the polygon vault. These vaults might have been less majestic than domes, but they were more picturesque and much more decorative. At York, built 1280–1330, there was no central column; the ceiling was a Gothic dome of wood 57 feet (17 m) in diameter.

When the central tower of Ely Cathedral collapsed and destroyed the choir, Alan of Walsingham built a magnificent octagon which occupied the width of the three aisles. It was a simple groined and ribbed vault constructed of wood which reached up to an octagonal lantern which could be seen externally as well as internally.

In the Early English Period, from about 1200 to 1275, windows were long and narrow and placed in groups of two to five. In Salisbury and Ely the aisles at the sides were lighted by pairs of windows, and the clerestory by groups of three, the centre one of which was longer than the others, a relic of Norman days.

At first the shape of the window openings formed the design, but later the shape of the openings was dictated by the design of the stone framework. Such stone tracery was general in England for a hundred years or so from about 1260 onwards. There was some resemblance to the geometric designs of the French, although the English tracery was less rigid and more varied. Early examples occurred in the cloisters at Salisbury, in the choirs of Lichfield, Lincoln and Ely, and also in the nave at York.

After this period, flowing tracery (lines of double curvature) was introduced, something like the French Flamboyant but simpler. Examples could be found in Wells, and also in the rose window of Lincoln. This, however, was only a transitional phase which soon gave way to the perpendicular style, in which the mullions were carried to the top of the arch and were intersected by horizontal transoms. This gave a rigid system of stone framing which did not have quite the grace and charm

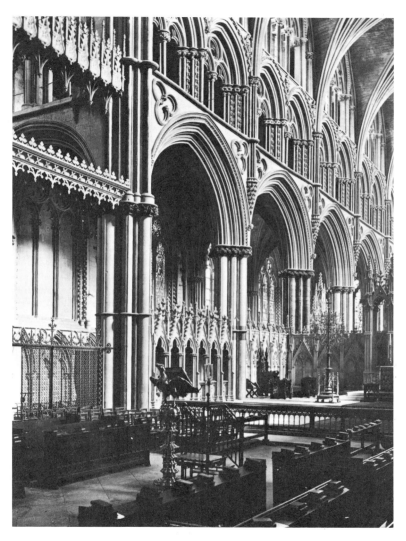

The 'Angel Choir' in Lincoln Cathedral.

of the earlier systems.

It was at about this time that the English appear to have accepted the Gothic ideas of emphasis on the vertical and reducing wall surfaces to an absolute minimum. Fan vaulting led to the adoption of a new form of arch, the four-centred or Tudor arch, which fitted under the depressed apex of the vault. Thus, internally and externally, the whole design was controlled by the form of the openings and of the vaultings. Windows were very large, and those at the square east end of the choir and over the entrance at the west were especially so. Thus in the *Perpendicular Period* the two ends of the church were almost entirely walls of glass. The East Window at Gloucester, for example, measured 38 by 72 feet (12 m × 22 m).

Generally speaking, the English were not able to match the majestic west fronts of Notre Dame, Amiens or Rheims, although the façades of York, Lincoln and Peterborough were interesting and outstanding in their make-up. The front of Lincoln was an arcaded screen which masked the bases of the two towers, and pierced three Norman arches left of the original façade. Salisbury had a most ineffective façade. Those at Lichfield and Wells were both beautiful designs, the former with its rich arcading and twin spires, and the latter with its huge towers and lovely figure-sculpture.

Perhaps one of the more successful elements of English design was provided by the central towers. Internally they formed lanterns and externally they were usually large, lofty and square. Completed mainly during the fourteenth and fifteenth centuries, they were rich in elegance and detail. Canterbury, Durham, York, Lincoln and Gloucester were good examples of these square central towers. Some had very high spires above the lantern; this at Salisbury rose 414 feet (126 m) and it was not completed until the fourteenth century. Lichfield and Chichester also had central spires and Norwich had a spire on its Norman tower.

In the Norman churches, the pier arches, the triforium and the clerestory each occupied one-third of the height. In Gothic churches we find that the pier arches took up half the height, the other half being divided between the triforium and the clerestory. This division was roughly equal at Lincoln, Lichfield and Ely, but at Winchester, Westminster and Salisbury the clerestory occupied more than the triforium. The English tended to introduce a large number of fine mouldings in the pier arches, to use elaborate decoration in the triforium, and to apply a variety of ideas in their treatment of the clerestory. In general, their interiors were far more ornate than those of the French. They often used

Black Purbeck marble for the shafts clustered round the core of the pier. The rich vaulting, the elaborately decorated triforium, the moulded pier arches and the effect of the great window at the east gave a very different impression from that of French cathedrals. The simple lofty stateliness of the French gave a picture of majesty and power, whereas the great length and lowness of the English with their decorative richness gave an impression of repose and grace.

During the *Early English Period* the detail of the carving was remarkably vigorous, and the foliage seemed to spring from the stone from which it was carved. Mouldings were frequently decorated in the hollows with foliage or with the dog-tooth ornament, thus bringing into the shadows of the mouldings repeated points of light. At this time cusping, that is the decoration of an arch or circle with triangular projections on its inner edge, became a means of decoration, especially in stone tracery.

In the *Decorated Period* the foliage became less crisp and vigorous. Often oak leaves and seaweed were closely bunched and used in capitals. It was then that geometric and flowing tracery developed, double curves were used in mouldings and hollows were not so frequently adorned with foliage.

The *Perpendicular Period* saw the coming of nearly every flat surface with minute panelling in designs which resembled the stone tracery of the windows. The mouldings became weaker and less effective, and the capitals were of less importance. At this time, also, the Tudor rose appeared as an ornament on flat surfaces and square panels. The amount of decorative ornament increased tremendously, but it had less variety and originality.

The parish churches made use of a great variety of plans, and many of them were of great beauty, and dated from the fourteenth and fifteenth centuries. Their square single west towers were typical, as were their carved wooden ceilings. The towers were built over the central west porch with corner buttresses crowned with pinnacles. Usually, they did not have a spire, but the upper storey was crowned by battlements. The square towers of note included those at Boston and St Nicholas, Newcastle.

Later, spires were added to square west towers. The transition from square tower to octagonal spire was made by means of portions of a square pyramid intersecting the base of the spire or by corner pinnacles and flying buttresses. Some of the spires of parish churches were exceptionally beautiful and were a successful feature of medieval architecture in England. The elaborate spires of later date at Louth, Patrington and St Michael's, Coventry, were considered to be outstanding architectural works, and that at Salisbury Cathedral was the most perfect of all English spires.

The English made use of woodwork with exceptional skill. They were able to invent and develop different forms of roof truss which combined the distribution of strains with decoration by the use of carving, moulding and arcading. The ceiling surfaces between the trusses were highly decorated, and many of the open timber ceilings of many English churches and indeed some civic or academic halls, such as Christ Church, Oxford, and Westminster Hall, London, were so beautiful as fully to justify the use of wood in place of vaulted ceilings. The hammerbeam truss was structurally and aesthetically the equal of any feature of French Gothic stone construction. Without the use of tie rods it put the strain of the roof on internal brackets low down on the wall and gave a very beautiful effect in repeating the graceful curves of each truss. Notable examples were the ceilings of parish churches at Wymondham, Trunch, March, St Stephen's Norwich, and also the Middle Temple Hall in London.

Many chapels and halls in England rivalled the cathedrals in their beauty and dignity. The royal chapels at Windsor and Westminster, and also King's College Chapel at Cambridge and Christ Church Hall at Oxford, should not be overlooked. The chapel of Merton College, Oxford, and that of St Stephen at Westminster were also outstanding. The Lady Chapels of Ely and Gloucester were remarkable for the richness of decoration and great windows and ribbed vaulting. The timber ceilings of some of the medieval castles and manor houses were also of outstanding beauty.

Generally speaking, the medieval castles of Great Britain came under the heading of military engineering, although occasionally there were some with features of architectural beauty. A period of peace and order was marked by the construction of manor houses for wealthy landowners. Many of them were imposing in size and showed the application of the Gothic style to domestic requirements. The windows were square or Tudor arched with stone mullions and horizontal transoms of the Perpendicular style. The walls terminated in parapets reminiscent of the earlier military structures.

Not many Gothic stone houses of the smaller type remain, but most old towns boast half-timbered houses of the fourteenth and fifteenth centuries in an excellent state of preservation. They were built on the same principle as those in France and the woodwork was richly carved. They tended to be wider and lower than the French ones.

Gothic architecture in Germany was introduced later than in France and England. Its development was slower and more provincial. The Germans were slow to abandon the imposing Romanesque ecclesiastical architecture and, as a result, there was a transition period of fifty years during which there was a mingling of Romanesque and Gothic. Still, in 1208, when St Castor at Coblenz was built, Romanesque designs were used entirely, and even when pointed arches and vaults were in general use the plans were predominantly Romanesque. They retained the short sanctuary and the western apse of the earlier plans. They had no triforium, an insignificant clerestory, and their entire structures were low and massive. The Germans avoided at first the audacity and difficulties of the French Gothic, but finally the influence of the French cathedrals and the employment of foreign architects persuaded the conservative Germans to domesticate the Gothic style. Most of the German Gothic work of the late fourteenth and fifteenth centuries displayed a technical cleverness and exaggeration of detail which became typical, as in the slender mullions at Ulm, and the complicated spire of Strasbourg.

The periods of the development of Gothic styles in Germany may be roughly divided as follows: the *Transitional*, from about 1170 to 1225, the *Early Pointed*, 1225–75, the *Middle* or *Decorated*, 1275–1350, and the *Florid*, 1350–1530. They were, however, less clearly defined than in France and in England and less uniform in the various provinces.

In Germany, however, more so than in any other part of Europe (except perhaps Italy), there was much more variety in the plans. Some churches retained the Romanesque short choir and second western apse. Generally, the Cistercian Churches had square east ends, whereas St Elizabeth at Marburg, Ulm Minster and Ratisbon Cathedral had the polygon eastern apse without an ambulatory. Magdeburg Cathedral, Altenburg, Cologne, Freiburg and Lübeck all had a single ambulatory and radiating apsidal chapels. Cologne Cathedral was the most magnificent and also the largest, and, being completely French in plan, united all the leading characteristics of French churches. It had double aisles through the nave and choir, three-aisled transepts, radial chapels and twin western towers.

In Germany they held on to Romanesque methods for a considerable time and preferred broad wall surfaces, small windows and low proportions to the more slender and lofty Gothic design. They stuck to square vaulting bays covering two aisle bays. Only rarely did they make use of the six-part system, and although they imported the idea of the ribbed vault it was never systematically developed.

In the second half of the thirteenth century, under the influence of French models, vaulting in oblong bays as at Freiburg, Cologne and Ratisbon Cathedrals became more general. During the fourteenth century a taste for elaborate and rich detail resulted in the use of multiplied decorative ribs, largely as decoration, but with all this richness the Germans developed nothing comparable to the English fan-vaulting, or chapter-house ceilings.

Many German churches had the side aisle vaults at the same height as that of the central vault. Thus the clerestory disappeared and the central aisle no longer dominated the interior. The pier arches and side walls were higher, and flying buttresses were unnecessary. The Cathedral of St Stephen in Vienna was an imposing instance of this hall-church idea.

The Germans displayed their fondness for spires in the Rhenish Romanesque churches, and during the Gothic period they produced many beautiful church steeples in which they substituted openwork tracery for the earlier solid stone pyramids. Examples of these spires appeared at Freiburg, Strasbourg and Cologne Cathedrals. The very elaborate spire at Strasbourg reached a height of 468 feet (143 m). The spires of Cologne, completed in 1883 from the original long-lost fourteenth century drawings, were 500 feet (152 m) high.

When German tracery followed the French patterns it was at its best. On its own it suffered from mechanical stiffness. The windows, especially in the hall churches, appeared too narrow for their height. In the fifteenth century grace of line gave way to ingenuity of geometric combinations. Later it took the form of boughs and twigs, interlaced and twisted.

Perhaps the earliest distinctive Gothic work in Germany was the Golden Portal of Freiburg, dated 1190. From then on Gothic details became more frequent, particularly in the Rhine provinces. Pointed arches and vaults appeared in the Apostles' and St Martin's Churches at Cologne, and the Church of St Peter and St Paul at Neuweiler had a purely Gothic nave. The Burgundian influence appeared in Magdeburg Cathedral in 1212, which imitated the choir of Soissons. Strasbourg Cathedral had its façade and its north spire designed after French models. The choir of Amiens was copied in Cologne Cathedral, which was begun in 1248, and the choir was consecrated in 1322. The nave and west front of Cologne were partly built in the fourteenth century, although the towers were not fully completed until 1880. Cologne

Cathedral, in spite of its size and slowness of construction, was in style the most uniform of all great Gothic cathedrals. Its details were, however, stiff and mechanical, and in its uniformity it lost the picturesque charm that usually results from a mixture of the styles of the work of many generations. Ratisbon Cathedral was one of the most beautiful and dignified of German Gothic churches; it was German in plan and French in execution. Many German hall-churches also show French influence in their detail.

In North Germany, where there was a lack of stone, the peculiarly German brick churches had flat walls and square towers, and they depended on coloured tiles and bricks for their decoration.

As in France and England, the fourteenth and fifteenth centuries were largely occupied in completing existing churches, many of which until then had been without naves. The building of spires went on at about the same time as the building of central square towers in England.

Germany completed a number of Gothic castles and municipal buildings. The first completely Gothic castle was not built until 1280 at Marienburg, and it was completed a hundred years later. Town halls at Ratisbon, Münster, Brunswick, Lübeck and Bremen dated from the fourteenth and fifteenth centuries.

Because of their geographic position, the Netherlands were largely under the influences of France and of Germany. Belgium came under the French influence, whereas Holland was more German in style. Of the two, perhaps Belgium's architecture became more interesting than that of the Dutch. The wealth and independent attitude of the Flemish weavers and merchants of the fifteenth century was reflected in the size and richness of the Flemish town halls and guildhalls.

The earliest purely Gothic structure was the choir at Ste Gudule at Brussels, 1225. The choir and transepts of Tournay which had side chapels and pointed vaults followed in 1242. Antwerp Cathedral had a seven-aisled nave and narrow transepts and had an area of 70,000 square feet (6510 m²). Its west front, which was built later, was rich and elegant and had a lofty and slender northern spire.

Of the Gothic town halls or guildhalls, the Cloth Hall at Ypres was the earliest (1200–1301), and perhaps the most imposing. Similar halls were built later at Bruges, Malines and Ghent. The town halls were of later date—Bruges was 1377 and Louvain 1448–63.

Generally speaking, Belgian architecture was purely that of a borrowed style. They did not change or develop it in any way, although there was a tendency to over-elaborate in the later work.

Town Hall at Mechelen, Belgium.

In Spain the beginnings of Gothic architecture followed closely on the campaigns of 1217–52 which began the overthrow of Moorish domination. The earliest purely Gothic churches in Spain were the cathedrals at Toledo and Burgos which were begun between 1220 and 1230. The former was planned in imitation of Notre Dame. It was wider, however, covered 75,000 square feet (6975 m²) and was one of the largest cathedrals in Europe. The west front of Burgos cathedral with its twin openwork spires suggested German influence, whereas the other thirteenth-century cathedrals of Leon, Valencia and Barcelona exhibited French influence in plan vaulting and high proportions. Bourges and Paris appeared to have been used as models for Barcelona Cathedral, for some fourteenth-century churches and also, as late as the sixteenth century, for the cathedral at Segovia. French influence also showed in Sta Maria del Pi at Barcelona, the nave of Gerona Cathedral and the collegiate church at Manreda. The Cathedral at Seville was begun in 1401, and was built on the site of a Moorish mosque. It measured 415 × 298 feet— 124,000 square feet (11,532 m²). It had five aisles, the central one 145 feet (44 m) high and 56 feet (17 m) wide, and the side aisles and chapels diminished in height gradually, making the six rows of piers quite imposing.

The fifteenth century throughout Europe tended towards over-decoration, and perhaps this was more the case in Spain than it was elsewhere. Decoration was less structural and much more fanciful. The Spanish architects delighted in broad wall surfaces and many horizontal lines, in contrast to the suppression of wall space and emphasis on vertical lines as in France and England, and on these surfaces they lavished carving of exquisite workmanship. The arcades of interior courtyards and cloisters were built with arches on twisted columns, and the chapels were covered with minute carving. Perhaps the influence of Moorish decoration contributed to some extent to the extravagance of the elaborate designs.

Gothic architecture was late in arriving in Portugal, but two convent churches at Batalha and Belem were outstanding, and both suffered from an excess of ornamental carving. The mausoleum of King Manuel at the back of Batalha church was of polygon shape and was 67 feet (20 m) in diameter. It was decorated with pinnacles and very profuse carving.

In Italy each province had followed its own style of Romanesque architecture and there was no uniformity of approach. The Italians were not attracted in any way to Gothic principles. They liked large wall spaces with small windows, which enabled them to secure space for mosaic decoration and wall paintings. Classic traditions persisted in their construction and in their decoration, their climate demanded small windows, thick walls and dim interiors instead of the vast Gothic windows. They liked the spaciousness and wide interiors which were typical of Roman design.

Finally, foreign influences resulted in the importation of Gothic fashions such as pointed arches and tracery, but somehow the detail still seemed to be Italian and also provincial. Rome built basilicas throughout the Middle Ages, Tuscany continued to build flat walls veneered with marble, Venice developed a Gothic façade of her own design—nowhere was there any real unity of approach. The round arch was used in conjunction with the pointed arch and the Roman acanthus and Corinthian capital were used frequently in their Gothic buildings.

It was the monastic orders who introduced Gothic forms into Italy, and perhaps it was the Cistercian Order who led the way in this. Some of their monasteries displayed French influences and dated from the early part of the thirteenth century. The Franciscans and the Dominicans built some of their churches with ribbed vaults and pointed arches and contributed in large measure to the final adoption of the Gothic style, which always retained an Italian twist. The church of S. Francesco at Assisi was the first Gothic Franciscan church. S. Andrea at Vercelli was very English in plan and had two western spires in the English manner. In every other respect, however, it was very Italian. The church at Asti suggested some German influence with its high side walls and narrow windows.

Italian cathedrals are all of imposing size. Milan, for example, is perhaps the largest Gothic cathedral, except for Seville. The Duomo, Sta Maria del Fiore, at Florence, begun in 1296, was finally given its large dome in 1420–64. It was 500 feet (152 m) long and its nave was 60 feet (18 m) wide. Its octagon measured 143 feet (44 m) in diameter, and it covered a total area of 82,000 square feet (7626 m²). As in so many cases its huge size accentuated the lack of detail and bareness of the huge walls, which they intended to cover with paintings and colour. Some outstanding examples of the splendour of such decoration were S. Francesco at Assisi, the Arena Chapel at Padua, and the Spanish Chapel of S. M. Novella at Florence. S. Petronia at Bologna was planned to be 600 feet (183 m) long, but only the nave of 300 feet (91 m) was constructed. It was divided into six bays, each of which had two side chapels, 46 feet (14 m) wide and 132 feet (40 m) high; its proportions approximated to those of the French cathedrals.

The Italians excelled themselves in the decoration of their pavements, pulpits, choir stalls and accessories generally. The exterior walls were mostly high and flat. Sometimes they were plain or striped with black and white masonry, or veneered with marble, and sometimes they were decorated with thin pilasters and arcades. The clerestorys were low, and the low pitched roofs were rarely visible from below. The façades were usually quite beautiful; and they had little relationship to the rest of the structure. The façades of Sienna Cathedral and of Orvieto were designed on similar lines. Each had three high gables with recessed portals, pinnacled turrets and a central circular window. They were executed in marble, and that of Orvieto was the more colourful as it was decorated with pictures in mosaic. The Ferrara Cathedral had a thirteenth-century, three-gabled and arcaded screen front. Externally, the most important feature was often a dome or a cupola over the crossing. Milan Cathedral externally had a spire 300 feet (91 m) high and a number of pinnacles. The Certosa at Pavia, built in 1396, had internal cupolas covered externally by a many-storeyed structure with a tower which dominated the whole. It was built of brick with moulded terracotta as the exterior ornamentation, and except for its ribbed vaulting had no Gothic features. The semi-classic arches, mouldings and cloisters were reminiscent of the Romanesque and Renaissance styles.

In the main the exterior decoration of Italian churches was largely panelled veneer of coloured marble and inlaid and mosaic patterns. A beautiful example of Italian Gothic art was in the campanile of the Duomo at Florence. Its inlays, mosaics and veneers and its incrusted reliefs were works of great elegance and beauty. The tracery of this structure was much lighter and more graceful than is usual in Italy. Venice developed tracery in her palaces more than any other city, and tracery in Italian secular monuments was usually more successful than that in their ecclesiastical structures.

In Italy the square tower was always preferred to the spire, and often it was an independent campanile. In accordance with Early Christian and Romanesque traditions they were often built with plain sides without buttresses and had a flat roof or just a low and inconspicuous cone or pyramid. The campaniles at Sienna, Lucca and Pistria were built like the adjoining cathedrals with alternate black and white courses. Those at Verona and Mantua had towers with octagonal lanterns. These towers differed from the Romanesque in their openings and detail of decoration.

In their domestic architecture, the Italians were able to apply Gothic forms without being hampered by traditional methods. In the northern cities pointed windows and open arcades were used to good effect. In Bologna and Sienna brick was used with moulded terracotta, and in Viterbo near Rome were built a number of interesting houses with street arcades, and open stairways leading to the main entrance.

The prosperity and security of Venice in the Middle Ages made massive and fortress-like architecture unnecessary, and domestic architecture favoured abundant openings, large windows and projecting balconies and use of marble veneer and inlay, which gave Venetian houses a typical air of elegance and gaiety not found elsewhere.

14
The Early Renaissance in Italy

The architecture of classical Rome had now lost its influence in Italy. Gothic art, which had never been wholly accepted in Italy, was on the decline, and the antique monuments which were everywhere were models which represented the glories of Ancient Rome. The Renaissance resulted in the abandoning of Gothic art in Italy and the adoption of forms derived from the classical models. There was a marked reaction against anything which affected the rights of the individual against the authority and teachings of the Church, and there was a questioning which led to the beginnings of modern science and the discoveries of early navigators. The Renaissance did in fact lay the foundations of modern civilization. There was a joy of living and love of beauty and pleasure which led to the enthusiastic pursuit of classical studies. There was a great awakening to the sense of personal freedom by the general throwing aside of the fetters of medieval scholarship and the fetters of external and arbitrary authority. Feudalism in Italy had never established itself fully and municipalities and guilds developed, there more than anywhere else, the sense of personal and civic freedom and a growing enthusiasm for everything reminiscent of the old classical culture.

The Italians longed to revive the beauty and glory of Ancient Rome, and in their enthusiasm appropriated indiscriminately both the good and bad of the various forms of Roman art. Unknown to themselves, by imitating the Roman and fitting it into their own ideas, they were in fact creating a new style. Increasingly, this new architecture entered into the building of palaces, villas, civic halls and monuments. As the Church lost its hold on culture, striking types of church design were created. The personal element of design played a great part in architectural development, and the history of architecture in Italy became the story of the achievements of individuals rather than of schools and styles.

During the thirteenth century, Niccolo Pisano in his pulpits at Sienna and Pisa had looked to the ancient monuments for inspiration. In many nominally Gothic buildings of the fourteenth century, classic forms had been repeatedly used. Florence, which was the artistic capital of Italy, was rich in artists who were quick to catch the spirit of the classical revival, and the new movement achieved its first real success in the construction of the dome of Florence Cathedral, 1420–64. It was Florentine artists who took the new art to Sienna, Milan, Bologna, Venice, and many other cities. The movement then took hold in Rome and in Naples.

The classic styles which grew up out of the Renaissance may be divided roughly into four periods: the Early Renaissance or Formative Period, the High Renaissance Period, the Baroque or Decline Period and the Classic Revival.

The *Early Renaissance* or *Formative Period*, about 1420 to 1490, was noted for its grace and the freedom of its detail, as suggested by classic Roman applied to new requirements in different combinations.

The *High Renaissance Period*, from about 1490 to 1560, followed. During this time classical orders and details were copied more closely, and the results were more stately, but also more stiff and less delicate.

Then came the *Baroque* or *Decline Period*, from about 1560 to 1700. In this period the orders were of colossal size; the decoration was scanty but heavy. There was much vulgar sham and display in its make-up.

Then came the *Classic Revival* during which there was a reaction against these extravagances and a return to imitating the old classical models, with a restraint in decoration and return of dignity.

The architects of the Renaissance were concerned with form rather than construction, and they tended to avoid problems of construction which might present difficulty. The new architecture began with the colossal dome of Florence Cathedral and ended with the stupendous achievement of St Peter's in Rome. It was mostly concerned with decorative display, façades, palaces and villas. If they met with difficulties of construction, they solved them in the simplest way possible. Any constructive framework was hidden by decoration and not emphasized. There were many small buildings, such as gates, chapels, tombs and fountains, which were considered as masterpieces of the Early Renaissance. Surprising results were achieved by the use of rich mouldings, carved friezes, wreaths of fruit, griffins, masks, scrolls, pilasters, inlays, carved doors, capitals, cornices, etc. There were free imitations of the Roman orders, with panelled and carved pilasters instead of columns, and fancy capitals with some slight Corinthian resemblance. Doors and windows were enclosed in frames which were sometimes square and sometimes arched, and they were richly carved. Generally, their façades were flat and unbroken and were decorated by the position and adornment of the windows, doors, mouldings and cornices. Inside, vaults and ceilings of wood and plaster were equally common in use. Nevertheless, the barrel vault and dome were used more frequently than the groined vault. Their ceilings were often of great beauty and richness.

The Duomo of Florence Cathedral was built between 1420 and 1464, and was made possible only as a result of a special study of Roman design and construction. It was not an imitation of Roman forms but was classic in its spirit, its huge size and its simple lines. It consisted of an octagonal dome in two shells connected by eight major and sixteen minor ribs, topped by a lantern. Brunelleschi, who designed the Duomo, also designed the Pazzi Chapel in the cloister of Sta Croce; this had a dome over the centre part.

The churches of S. Lorenzo, 1425, and S. Spirito, 1433-76, were also erected from Brunelleschi's designs. They were really basilicas with transepts and dome-vaulted side aisles. The central aisles were covered with flat ceilings and a low dome was built over the crossing. The domes were Byzantine rather than Roman, yet all the details were imitations of Roman and the result was something entirely new.

From this time a new style came into general use for the design of churches, and L. B. Alberti, who had really mastered classic Roman details, remodelled the church of S. Francesco at Rimini with Roman pilasters and arches and engaged orders in the façade. The church of S. Andrea at Mantua, which was a Latin cross in plan, and had a dome at the intersection and a façade in which a Roman triumphal arch was adapted, was Alberti's great work.

Between 1475 and 1490 there was great activity in church building. The plans of churches built about this time had a variety of arrangements, but in nearly all a dome was combined with the three-aisled cruciform plan. Sometimes the basilican arrangement was followed with arcades of columns separating the aisles. More frequently, however, the pier arches were Roman with engaged columns or pilasters in between. Generally, the interiors intended for printed decoration were still bare of ornament. The exteriors too were somewhat bare of decoration, except the façades which were often very ornate. The doorways with their columns, sculpture and carving were highly decorative. High external domes did not come into general use until the next period. In Milan and Pavia, however, the internal cupola was covered externally by a lofty structure with diminishing storeys, as in the Certoza at Pavia, or that in the church of S.M. delle Grazie at Milan. Some of the smaller churches, which were very successful in design, were of Greek cross type with four short barrel-vaulted arms projecting from the central area, which was covered by a dome of moderate height.

The architects of the Early Renaissance were most successful in their designing of chapels and oratories, as they presented fewer structural difficulties and were more decorative in character than the larger churches. The façades of S. Bernardino at Perugia and of the Frati di S. Spirito at Bologna were delightful examples of the decorative beauty of the art of the fifteenth century.

Early Renaissance architects achieved real success in their palaces. The Riccardi Palace in Florence had a very imposing rectangular façade. It had widely spaced mullioned windows in two storeys, with a huge basement. It was topped by a classic cornice of unusually excessive size, and gave an impression of a bold and fortress-like structure. The courtyard in contrast to the stern exterior appeared light and cheerful. Around the courtyard the walls were carried on round arches supported by columns with Corinthian type capitals. The Strozzi Palace also in Florence followed the type of the Riccardi Palace and was one of the noblest of all the palaces in Italy.

These palaces were built around central courts, with the walls resting on the columns of arcades. These arcades originated in the cloisters of medieval monastic churches which often suggested classical models. Columnar arcades were introduced into a number of palace courtyards but they were also used to good effect externally as at the Foundling Hospital and the Loggia S. Paolo, also in Florence.

In Sienna between 1450 and 1490 a number of Renaissance palaces were built in marked contrast to the predominantly Gothic architecture of that city. The P. del Govero was built in 1469, and the Spanocchi Palace in 1470. In Lucca the P. Pretorio and the P. Bernardini were built. Bologna and Ferrara developed their own local style, using brick and terracotta, in the P. Bevilacqua and P. Fava in the former city, and P. Scrofa and P. Roverella in the latter. Palaces were erected also in Verona, Mantua and other cities, with the interior courtyard arcades and other details of the new style.

Venice, because of the wealth of its inhabitants and its contacts with the East, was fond of splendour and display. The Gothic style coloured with Byzantine decorative ideas had adapted itself well to the needs of the people. The Renaissance architects therefore continued to make use of existing traditions at the same time as they introduced details of the new style. The church of S. Zaccaria, built between 1456 and 1515, was partially Gothic inside, but its façade with its decorative arcades gave a hint of the classic. It was highly decorative throughout and the mouldings, reliefs, capitals and other ornaments were most graceful and delicate.

The court of the Doge's Palace in Venice attracted admiration for the variety and picturesque effect of its decoration. From an architectural aspect the façade of the P. Vendramini was much more satisfactory and was perhaps outstanding among the palaces of Italy.

Because of civil disorders and the exile of the popes, the importance of Rome had diminished very considerably by the end of the fourteenth century. It was not until later in the fifteenth century that the Renaissance had any chance of getting a foothold in Rome, with a return of prosperity and wealth to the city. In 1450 Pope Nicholas V began rebuilding St Peter's, but the project lapsed with his death soon afterwards. Perhaps the first Renaissance building in Rome was the P. di Venezia which was begun in 1455. The arcade of the inner court was built like those in the Colosseum with massive piers and engaged columns.

In time the new style supplemented the basilican traditions of the Church, and in the churches of S. Agostino and of S.M. del Popolo were piers with pilasters and massive arches which separated the aisles, and the whole was topped with a dome.

Among the town halls built during this period was the P. del Consiglio at Verona. The façade had a graceful arcade which supported a wall pierced with four windows. The Ducal Palace at Urbino had a fine arcaded courtyard and was built in about 1468.

As time went on, the study of Roman architecture led to a closer copying of the details of the system, and the old classical orders were made more and more use of externally, in the decoration of wall openings and also in the inner court arcades. The dome crowned with a lantern and standing on a high drum was developed with remarkable effect. Interior decoration became more rich than ever and vaults and ceilings were painted by leading artists, as in the P. del Té at Mantua by Giulio Romano, and the Sistine Chapel in Rome by Michelangelo. During this period there were many great architects who constructed a large number of palaces, villas and churches. The construction of St Peter's at Rome was begun, and there was a complete transformation in the appearance of Rome itself. Two of the outstanding architects of this period were Bramante (1444–1514) and Michelangelo (1475–1564). The former ushered in the period of the Renaissance whereas the latter may be said to have closed it. Bramante's early work included the S.M. delle Grazie, the sacristy of San Satiro, and the extension of the Great Hospital in

Milan. It was his later work which clearly showed a tendency towards the classic. In 1506 Bramante began the rebuilding of St Peter's for Pope Julius II and also the building of a palace adjoining it. He built the greater Belvedere Court, the lesser octagonal court and the court of San Damiso with its arcades. He also built the cloister of S.M. della Pace and many other works.

The Palaces of Rome were usually very large and were built around inner courts with two or three storeys of classic arcades. The two or three storeyed façade was topped with a rich cornice. The classical orders were used only sparingly externally. The first storey above the basement consisted of reception rooms and halls, and the ceilings and frescoes were painted by the foremost artists of the time, while much use was made of statues and reliefs for the decoration of the courts, vestibules and niches. Perhaps the finest palace in Italy was the Farnese Palace; its construction was begun in 1530. Its cornice was by Michelangelo. Its vaulted vestibule, the inner court and the salons were well worthy of the great architects who participated in its design.

The Italian villas enabled the architects, decorators and landscape gardeners to 'let themselves go'. Each villa usually consisted of a house, a casino or amusement house, summer houses, arcades etc. and, of course, the gardens. An outstanding example of this beautiful combination of skills was the Villa d'Este at Tivoli.

The earlier churches of this period usually had a dome as a central feature which dominated a cruciform plan, whereas the exteriors were in the main simple and uninteresting. The culmination of Renaissance church architecture, however, was in the rebuilding of St Peter's, Rome. Bramante, who designed it, died in 1514; and the collapse of two arches under the dome and delays due to Bramante's death resulted in the plan being abandoned until Michelangelo was given the work in 1546, but he died in 1564. The huge dome, which measured 140 feet (43 m) in diameter and rose to a height of 405 feet (123 m) at the top of the lantern, was finally completed in 1604.

In 1606 the nave was lengthened by two bays and the portico was added in 1629–67. It was the largest church in the world and its central aisle was nearly 600 feet (183 m) long.

By the middle of the sixteenth century the classic orders dominated architectural design. The churches in which a Greek or Latin cross was dominated by a high dome topped by a lantern, and which were decorated inside and outside with Corinthian pilasters and arches, were built all over Italy. Included among churches of this type were the Gesù in

Rome (1568), the St Giorgio Maggiore (1560) and the Redentore in Venice, and the S.M. di Barigneno at Genoa, begun in 1552.

The palace architecture of this period may be illustrated by those built on the Capitoline Hill between 1540 and 1644 from designs by Michelangelo. Perhaps the most successful was the Palace of Caprarola near Rome. Outside Rome, Michele Sammichele, 1484–1554, built the Bevilacqua, Canossa, Pompeii and Verzi Palaces in Verona. He also built the chief city gates, and the P. Grimani in Venice (1550). In Venice, also, Giacopo Tatti Sansovino made use of coupled columns between arches which were supported by columns, and figure sculpture made the façades of his palaces really magnificent.

Vicenza was a native of the city of Palladio and most of the palaces built by him were found in that city. He was extremely inventive and was very familiar with the classic orders, but his work began to show signs of the degeneracy of the Baroque and his palaces generally did not have the grace of those of Vignola and Sammichele. His one outstanding masterpiece was the two-storeyed arcade which he built round the medieval basilica in Vicenza. In it the arches were supported on a minor order between engaged columns serving as buttresses.

In Genoa, during the second half of the sixteenth century, a number of palaces with huge courts and imposing staircases were built. Because they were built on a slope on a hillside the courts were of different levels, which gave the staircases unusual prominence.

A reaction to the formal classic style of the late sixteenth century set in with the tasteless extravagance of the Baroque style. The Jesuit order, which was extremely wealthy, contributed in large measure to the degeneration of architectural taste. Wood and plaster was used to imitate stone and marble and gilding was carried to excess. The Baroque style persisted in church architecture for nearly two hundred years; during that time, however, there were some churches which were exceptions to the general tasteless standard. Naples, for example, had many Baroque churches, yet among them the Gesù Nuovo (1584) was outstanding. The S.M. della Salute (1631) in Venice was also a magnificent exception. A number of churches during this period suffered by remodelling; these included the cathedrals at Palermo, Ravenna and many others.

Generally speaking, the Baroque palaces were more dignified and more impressive than the churches. The P. Borghese and the P. Barberini in Rome were among the best examples.

During this period, also, many of the fountains in Rome, Florence, Bologna and Messina etc. were erected; the Fonte Felice and the Fonte

Paolina in Rome were among these.

During the eighteenth century there was some reaction to the extravagances of the previous century, and the exteriors of buildings appeared to be more dignified, whereas the interiors were less rich in their splendour. The Royal Palace at Caserta (1752) was an excellent work. It was 800 feet (244 m) square and had four inner courts. Its exterior was one of simple dignity and had three octagonal vestibules, a grand staircase and an ornate chapel. Among the churches of this period, the east front of S. John Lateran (1734) and the exterior of S.M. Maggiore (1743) were worthy of particular note. The Fountain of Trevi (1735) should also be mentioned.

The campaniles of the Renaissance in Italy were of less importance than other types of architecture. Some were merely square towers with pilasters, whereas others had engaged columns and entablatures which marked the storeys, and the upper part was topped by a lantern, with diminishing stages or with a spire. Perhaps the most perfect of those square campaniles was the Campidoglio in Rome.

The actual revival of the ancient Roman forms was only for brief periods, during the latter half of the sixteenth century, and in a few buildings during the eighteenth century. The architects of the Early Renaissance did not achieve their objective of really reviving Roman art, and those during the Decline soon tired of its inherent restrictions, perhaps largely because of the automatic copying of the classic forms by their predecessors.

15
Renaissance—France

The richness and popularity of the Gothic style greatly delayed the acceptance of the ancient classic forms. When it did come it was introduced largely by the king and the nobility from Italy. For a time the traditional French Gothic forms were mixed with details of the Renaissance. Charles VIII (1489) and his successors Louis XII (1499) and Francis I (1515), in their claims for the throne of Naples and dukedom of Milan, came into direct contact with the splendid magnificence of the Italian Renaissance, and returned to France with Italian artists in an endeavour to emulate the beautiful palaces and gardens of Italy. The Italians were able to introduce many classical elements into French architecture, but they were unable to change the French artisans in their ways of building. So early French Renaissance, although it derived details from the Italian, was very different. It was royal and courtly, and dominated by the taste and wishes of the monarchs who introduced it.

The French Renaissance may be divided into three main periods, with sub-divisions largely corresponding to various reigns, as follows:

1. *The Renaissance proper* (1483–1589).
   a) The Transition, the reign of Charles VIII, Louis XII and the early years of Francis I.
   b) Early Renaissance, 1520–47 (the death of Francis I).
   c) Advanced Renaissance, Henry II (1547), Francis II (1559), Charles IX (1560) and Henry III (1574–89).
2. *The Classic Period* (1589–1715).
   a) Style of Henry IV covering his reign and part of that of Louis XIII (1610–43).
   b) Style of Louis XIV (1643–1715).
3. *The Decline or Rococo Period* (the reign of Louis XV, 1715–74).

In church architecture, Gothic forms continued for a long time, notwithstanding the large number of Italian prelates in France. The new style made an early appearance in church accessories such as altars, rood screens and tombs. In this work there was some collaboration between the French carvers and Italian artisans; the tomb erected by Charles of Anjou to his father in Le Mans Cathedral (1475) and the tomb of the children of Charles VIII in Tours Cathedral (1506) were excellent examples.

It was, however, in non-church structures that the new style succeeded. The castle of Charles VIII at Amboise showed no trace of any Italian influence, and it was not until the reign of Louis XII that any changes were noticeable. The Château de Gallion, built between 1497 and 1509, notwithstanding its Renaissance details, retained in its irregular plan, moat, drawbridge and round corner towers a medieval character. The Château de Blois, begun about 1500 for Louis XII, showed the new style in its horizontal lines and flat façades of brick and stone.

Under Francis I, Gothic details began to be replaced by classic elements, and a simple method of exterior design came to be adapted for castles and palaces. Finely moulded courses marked the storeys at the window sills and window heads, crossed by pilasters on each side of the windows continuously from the ground to the roof. The façade was topped by a cornice and open balustrade, above which was a steep and high roof which had dormer windows with gables and pinnacles. Slender pilasters with graceful Corinthian type capitals were used in preference to columns. The mouldings were small and richly carved, and mullioned windows with stone cross-bars were preferred to the Italian style openings. Until a late date, round corner towers, turrets and pinnacles and other Gothic details continued to be used.

Under Francis I, ecclesiastical architecture remained Gothic. The Church of St Etienne du Mont in Paris (1517-38) incorporated classic and Gothic form; the plan and construction of St Eustrache (1532), also in Paris, was entirely Gothic, yet the actual details were in the new style. The Gothic towers of Tours Cathedral were completed with Renaissance lanterns in 1507 and 1547.

Francis I added a northern and western wing to the palace at Blois. The inner façade of the north wing was divided by an open Staircase Tower which was noted for its bold construction and the richness of its carving. The Palace at Fontainebleau was larger than Blois. Its interior was perhaps the most magnificent in France.

Perhaps the most important of the architectural constructions of this time was the beginning of the new palace to replace the old Louvre which had been a Gothic fortified palace. The work started in 1546. It was to have covered the same area as the old fortress, but only two sides of the court were undertaken at first, and it remained for later monarchs to complete what became the largest and most beautiful of all royal residences in Europe.

Among other outstanding buildings constructed about this time was the Hôtel-de-Ville in Paris, and also the town hall of Beaugency. Mention should also be made of the Maison Francis I which was originally erected at Moret, and in 1830 was transported to Paris and re-erected.

By the middle of the sixteenth century, the orders were being used more and more, arches were more Roman in their execution, and the carving was heavier. During the reigns of Henry II and Charles IX from 1547 to 1574, there were three celebrated architects. Pierre Lescet (1515–78) continued the work on the Louvre. Jean Bullant (1515–78) built the right wing of the Ecouen and the porch of its left wing, and Philibert de l'Orme (1515–70) worked on the Tuileries Palace and also the Château d'Anet.

There was much architectural activity under Henry IV and his Florentine queen, who with his Italian prelates had a considerable influence on the style, which had a touch of Baroque. The Luxembourg Palace was built for the Queen in 1616. The main building was separated from the street by a court which was surrounded on three sides.

During the reign of Louis XIII the Tuileries were extended and the Louvre was doubled in size. At about the same time the church of St Paul-St Louis was built; it had the earliest internal dome in Paris. The chapel of the Sorbonne with its dome was begun in 1635. In the same style were the churches of St Roch and St Sulpice. Internally these churches had dignity and simplicity. They were built in stone but, lacking painted decoration, were rather cold and severe.

The reign of Louis XIV saw great activity. Although it coincided with the Baroque period in Italy, it was free from the same extravagances. In contrast it was often coldly correct and made great use of the orders. Much use was made internally of relief ornaments such as scrolls, wreaths and wall panelling. The Galerie d'Apollon in the Louvre illustrated this type of treatment.

The Palace of Versailles was built by Levau (1612–70) and Mansart (1647–1708). Together with the marvellous park, it was of vast size. It contained the famous Hall of Mirrors which was one of the most magnificent halls in Europe.

The Louvre was completed in 1688. The east front had an immense Corinthian colonnade 600 feet (183 m) long with coupled columns. Its

The Grand Trianon at the palace of Versailles, France.

façade was most imposing. It was a stately palace of great dignity and beauty, unrivalled by any other structure save that of the Vatican.

The Hôtel des Invalides was also built in the reign of Louis XIV and the celebrated dome was added to its chapel in 1680–1706. During this period also were built the early part of the Palais Royal, the Hôtel Lambert on the Ile St Louis and the extension of the Hôtel Carnavalet.

Under Louis XV, the façade of St Sulpice was built in 1755 and the Panthéon with its dome was begun in that same year; it was perhaps the greatest French ecclesiastical monument of its time. Its portico had eighteen large Corinthian columns and its double aisles were separated by columns of the same order. The centre dome, which was 60 feet (18 m) in diameter, was surrounded by a magnificent colonnade. A great deal of attention was paid to the adornment of open spaces in the cities, and the classic style was well suited. Outstanding in this respect was the north side of the Place de la Concorde in Paris, which had two colonnades with pavilions at each end.

Under Louis XVI there developed a period of puritan severity in decoration both internally and externally. There were not many great structures erected during this time.

Generally speaking, the architecture of the French Renaissance was outstanding for its good proportions. It was most successful in its treatment of roofs, dormers, chimneys and staircases and it steadily advanced in its mastery of planning.

16
Renaissance—Great Britain

During the reigns of Henry VII and Henry VIII much of the architectural activity was confined to the building of large country mansions for the nobility and wealthy landowners. The building style, which retained aspects of the feudal Middle Ages, was a degenerate form of Gothic which became known as the Tudor style. It was typified by broad square windows and large halls. The earlier parts of Hampton Court and the castles of Raglan and Wolterton were built at this time.

In the reign of Elizabeth I (1558–1603) the importation of Dutch and Italian artists resulted in a gradual use of Renaissance ideas mixed with Gothic. Slowly the pointed arch disappeared and the orders were used more and more frequently in the decoration of wall-openings, chimneys, etc. The heavy Tudor battlements were replaced by open-work balustrades. The orders were used at Wollaton Hall (1580) with mullioned windows as at Longleat House a year earlier. The Gate of Honor of Caius College, Cambridge, Burghley and Hatfield House were examples of the style used at that time.

The orders and other classic details came into general use during the reign of James I (1603–25), but a number of the great manor-houses retained some of the charm of the Elizabethan period.

Inigo Jones (1572–1652) was really the first to introduce the style of the Italians' classic designs and he designed a villa at Chiswick which was a smaller version of Palladio's Villa Capra near Vicenza. He had a great regard for Palladio and his work. He designed the Palace of Whitehall but completed only the Banqueting Hall. The palace if completed would have measured 1152 feet by 720 feet (351 m × 219 m). The Banqueting Hall had two storeys and was adorned with columns and pilasters. Inside was a vaulted hall which had three aisles. He built Wilton House, Coleshill, St Paul's, Covent Garden, and the garden-front of Somerset House.

Sir Christopher Wren (1632–1723) was known principally for St Paul's Cathedral in London, which he built to replace the earlier Gothic cathedral burned down in the Great Fire of 1666. The new cathedral was

Tombland Alley, Norwich.

completed in 1710 and was English Gothic in proportions. Its dome was 216 feet (66 m) in height and the cathedral was 480 feet (146 m) long and the transepts 250 feet (76 m). The rotunda was 108 feet (33 m) in diameter. Externally there were two storeys of the Corinthian order, the upper one being used as a screen for the clerestory. The west front had a two-storey porch and bell-turrets on each side. The eight arches supporting the dome occupied the width of the three aisles.

Wren designed many of the parish churches of London, outstanding among which was St Stephen's Walbrook, which had a dome supported by eight columns. Bow Church, Cheapside, had a spire on a square tower the style of which (attributed to Wren) was described as the English Renaissance type of steeple. In all, Wren designed fifty-one churches, as well as royal palaces and public buildings. He did not work as an architect until comparatively late in life. He started off as a scientist and an astronomer. A founder member of the Royal Society, he was at twenty-nine Professor of Astronomy at Oxford. Although Wren had never visited Rome, his work was definitely influenced by the Baroque style, which he modified to suit his own ideas. Wren made great use of craftsmen of all nationalities. In building St Paul's, for example, he employed a team of outstanding craftsmen, which included the master woodcarver Gibbons, the Danish sculptor Gibber and the French metalworker Tijon.

The Anglo-Italian style developed and used by Jones and Wren was continued during the eighteenth century by the leading architects of the time, included among which were Vanbrugh (1666–1726), Hawksmoor (1666–1736) and Gibbs (1683–1754). Vanbrugh designed Blenheim and Castle Howard. Hawksmoor produced St Mary's Woolnoth in London (1715), St George's Bloomsbury and the quadrangle at All Souls Oxford. Gibbs was noted for St Martin-in-the-Fields in London (1726). He also built the Radcliffe Library, Oxford (1747).

The principal architects of the eighteenth century were: Sir William Chambers (1726–96), who extended and remodelled Inigo Jones' Somerset House, adapting it to a frontage of 600 feet (183 m); Robert Adam, who designed Edinburgh University and also Keddlestone Hall; the Dances, who designed the Mansion House and Newgate Prison in London; and Sir John Soane who was responsible for the Bank of England.

17
Renaissance—Belgium, Holland, Denmark

The Gothic style in Belgium had been highly developed and the Renaissance forms were slow in being accepted. It was not until about 1530–40 that the earliest Renaissance buildings appeared. They included the Hôtel du Saumon in Malines, the Ancien Griffe in Bruges, and the Archbishop's Palace in Liège, which latter clearly showed the influence of Spanish artists, as from 1506 to 1712 Belgium was ruled by Spain and there was an exchange of artists during that period.

Perhaps the most important Renaissance structure in Belgium was the Hôtel de Ville, erected in Antwerp (1565) by Cornelius de Vriendt, with a façade 305 feet (93 m) long and 102 feet (31 m) high. It had four storeys with an open colonnade under the roof, and an open arcade forming the basement. Amongst other things de Vriendt designed the rood-screen in Tournay Cathedral.

There was nothing outstanding about Flemish ecclesiastical architecture during the Renaissance. Typical was St Anne in Bruges, the detail of which was heavy, whereas internally there was a coldness and bareness. Perhaps the best examples of the Renaissance in Belgium were in minor works, which included ordinary houses with their stepped gables and high dormers.

The Renaissance in Holland came with the work of Flemish and Italian artists. About the middle of the sixteenth century, van Zoye and van Noort remotely imitated Francis I by using carved pilasters and decorating gables with carved scallop shells. Perhaps the main building activity was in town halls, and when Holland achieved independence from Spain (1566–70) there was a considerable amount of construction of administrative buildings. The Town Hall at The Hague with its octagonal turrets was among these. Because of a general lack of stone, brick had to be used, and only for buildings of importance was stone imported at heavy cost. The Town Hall at Amsterdam was among the latter.

The Renaissance in Denmark was largely confined to 1588–1648, the reign of King Christian IV. During this period the Rosenborg, the

Christianborg and the Fredericksborg were built. They were all royal castles, with gables, mullioned windows and many turrets. There were no churches of any importance built during that time.

Characteristic gabled house in Zaandijk, Holland.

18
Renaissance—Austria, Germany, Spain, Portugal

Before the end of the fifteenth century, Italian architects from Florence and Milan were being employed in Austria, Bohemia and the Tyrol, and a number of palaces and chapels were built in the Italian style. The portal of the castle at Mahrisch-Trübau was built in 1492. The Schloss Porzia at Spital, which was built in 1510, had a court with arcades on three sides. The Imperial Palace at Vienna (1562) and others can all be attributed to Italian architects.

The Renaissance had no effect on German architecture until after 1555, when it made rapid progress confining itself mainly to castles, town halls and houses for the wealthy. Because of the Reformation, church architecture was neglected. The periods of Renaissance architecture in Germany were less defined than those in France, but followed the same development in three stages.

1. *Early Renaissance* (from about 1525 to 1600). Most structures had a Gothic touch. The orders were, however, occasionally used for porches and the decoration of gables.
2. *Late Renaissance* (from 1600 to 1675) displayed a heavy treatment making use of broken curves, large scrolls and obelisks reminiscent of Elizabethan. Occasionally a more correct classic treatment after the Italian style was used.
3. The *Decline* or *Baroque* (1675 to 1800). The orders were used in a style which varied between the extremes of bareness and over-decoration. The details clearly showed the influence of Louis XV and the Italian Jesuits.

Generally speaking, the characteristics of German Renaissance architecture were the high roofs, stepped gables and lofty dormers which had been handed down from medieval times. They did not make much use of the orders, and when they did they were far too large and heavily ornamented. The plans did not have the huge size and symmetry of those of the Italian and French, and often their courtyards were irregular in shape and embellished with balconies and turrets with spiral

145

Baroque façade in Innsbruck, Austria.

146

staircases. Their interior decoration was more successful. Many of their ceilings were outstanding, and were panelled, painted, and gilded.

The German castles of the princes and dukes retained many medieval features during the Renaissance, both in plan and in general appearance. Many of them were actually built on the foundations of ancient feudal castles, reproducing in a more modern dress the old round towers and vaulted halls as in the Hartenfels at Torgau and the Heldburg and the castle of Trausnitz. However, the portal of the Heldburg built in 1562 was largely influenced by the current French style.

A number of castles and palaces built at the end of the sixteenth and beginning of the seventeenth centuries did not include any trace of feudal traditions and were of more regular design. Built around rectangular courts, they had arcades on two or three storeys usually on one or two sides of the courtyards. These arcades were on short Ionic or Corinthian columns supporting segmental arches. Usually a large and lofty banqueting hall dominated over all. Usually also there were no corridors, the rooms running into each other. The earliest of these castles and palaces were of Italian design; these included the Residenz at Landshut, with a purely Roman plan with its exterior façade and court decorated with the orders.

The Plassenburg (1554–64) made use of the segmental arch and stumpy columns in the German taste. Heidelberg Castle had an irregular plan and medieval aspect. The early parts of its wings were Gothic.

Many of the town halls were built in solid blocks without courts and were adorned with towers. They usually had a high roof broken by high gables or many-storeyed dormers. The town hall at Bremen (1612) had a beautiful exterior arcade on Doric columns. The one at Nuremberg was unusual as it did have a court, and had a façade of almost Roman simplicity.

Of the churches, St Michael's of Munich, built in 1582 during the first period, must be noted. It had a wide nave flanked by side chapels, separated by large piers. It had short transepts and a choir, all in good proportion. Typical of the parish churches of the second period was the Marienkirche of Wolfenbüttel built in 1608. It had pointed arches and a square tower.

As regards German houses in the sixteenth and seventeenth centuries, Nuremberg and Hildesheim had some excellent examples, built either for private use or for guilds and corporations. Some were half timbered and others were built entirely of stone.

During the third period the elaborate Zwinger Palace was built in

Dresden (1711-22), and the Marienkirche also in Dresden was an excellent example of late Renaissance; externally it was dignified and its proportions were good. Internally, however, the effect was rather theatrical.

The Germans were not particularly prolific in minor works. One tomb, however, was outstanding—the Sebald Shrine in Nuremberg (1506-19), which was executed in the transitional style in bronze. There were also a number of fountains in the squares of cities which were of excellent design.

In Spain the Gothic style met the requirements of the period which followed the defeat of the Moors and the discovery of America. However, the employment of Flemish and Italian artists did in time have an effect on the arts. The importation of silver from the New World led to a boost in the design of decorative jewellery, with its minute detail. This type of decoration lent itself to the surrounds of wall openings, pilasters and carved balusters. This profusion of minute ornament, however, was succeeded by a classic style which lasted until the seventeenth century. In the churches for a time there was a tendency towards extravagance of design and detail, but in about the middle of the eighteenth century the coming to Spain of a number of Italian architects swung the pendulum back to the classic style.

The early ecclesiastical works in Spain during the Renaissance period were, as in Salamanca and Segovia Cathedrals, mainly Gothic. However, Jaen Cathedral (1525) with three aisles and side chapels was entirely Corinthian order inside. The large and dignified cathedral of Granada (1529) had a domed sanctuary 70 feet (21 m) wide. Malaga Cathedral, the Church of San Domingo and San Girolamo Monastery, both of Salamanca, had portals which were especially rich in decoration, and that of San Girolamo almost forms the entire façade. The detailed carving of the portal of the University of Salamanca showed Italian and French influence in its execution. The Spaniards had a preference for long façades of moderate height, with the decoration largely concentrated around the doors and windows and often in elaborate roof balustrades. Occasionally a decorative motive was spread over the entire façade as in the Casa de las Conchas at Salamanca which had carved cockle shells at intervals over the front. The courtyard or patio was a feature of these buildings; it was usually surrounded by an arcade heavily decorated with minute detail as in the Infantada Palace at Guadalajara.

The introduction of the use of the orders ushered in a period of classic treatment of architectural design. Alonzo Berruguete (1480-1561) studied in Italy and he built the Archbishop's Palace and the Doric Gate of San Martino in Toledo. He also built the first royal palace in Madrid. The Valladolid Cathedral built by Juan de Herrara, under Philip V, was constructed on the same general lines as Jaen and Granada but was severely and classically correct. The Monastery of the Escurial begun in 1563 was not completed for nearly 150 years. It was a huge rectangle measuring 740 feet by 580 feet (226 m × 177 m) consisting of courts, halls and cells, dominated by a huge domed chapel which covered 70,000 square feet (6510 m^2) treated throughout with the Doric order.

The Palace at Madrid, which was rebuilt after it was burned down in 1734, was mainly the work of an Italian—Ivara.

Generally speaking, the ecclesiastical buildings of this period were executed in extravagantly bad taste, but they still had a picturesque attraction. Extreme examples of this style were built in Mexico and Arizona during the seventeenth and eighteenth centuries. Perhaps the best features of Spanish churches during this period were the towers, which were usually placed in pairs at the west end.

The skill of the Spanish artists in decorative design showed itself in many tombs and in rood screens, in which considerations of construction did not place any restrictions on the imagination.

In Portugal the Renaissance did not produce many outstanding examples of architecture of this period. Perhaps the best were at Belem in the Tower, the church and the cloister. The work was beautifully done and consisted of minutely carved detail in great profusion freely mingled with late Gothic features (1500–40). The Royal Palace at Mafra rivalled in its size and dignity the Escurial in Madrid; it was built by a German architect (1717–30).

19
Neo-Classic

The Renaissance came to an end in Europe before the beginning of the eighteenth century. Popular taste had grown tired of the restraints of the classic style and had welcomed the extravagance of the Baroque, of which in turn they tired. With the growth of industry and commerce in the eighteenth century, together with the many political changes which occupied people's attention, there was a tendency for a turning back to the safer and more comfortable classic architectural forms. It resulted in a pure copying of the Roman arcades and porticos, as façades for buildings whose modern requirements had to adjust themselves to their classic period exteriors. This resulted in a general improvement in the grandness of the streets and squares with such decorative façades, perhaps to the detriment of the ability of the buildings to fulfil their practical purposes. The architecture of the Roman Revival, although grand and artificial, was perhaps an improvement on the dullness or extravagance of the styles it displaced.

In France the Classic Revival first appeared during the reign of Louis XV. The Grand Théâtre at Bordeaux, built in 1785, was an example of the belief that only by closely and correctly copying the forms of Roman architecture could the grandeur of Rome be recreated. The colonnades of the Garde-Meuble, the façade of St Sulpice, and the beautiful Panthéon all testified to this belief. Under Louis XVI there was a temporary halt to this tendency to assume the ancient grandeur, and there were few important buildings during this period. Under Napoleon, however, the Roman Revival really came back. The Arc de Triomphe, the Arc de l'Etoile and the church of the Madeleine were all designed under the orders of Napoleon to be as Roman as it was possible to make them. The Madeleine was externally a Roman Corinthian temple and all its details were Roman. All of these designs were excellent in workmanship and elegant in detail. They added considerably to the splendour and magnificence of the French capital, although perhaps their design was not always appropriate to their intended use. There was, however, no doubt about the fact that Greek or Roman colonnades were the ideal embellishment of broad avenues and open squares.

Although the Roman Revival under Louis XV had produced some notable results, and the École des Beaux Arts had perpetuated the principles of Roman design, the Greek Revival made little impact, as Greek forms were thought to be too severe for modern requirements. However, about 1830, a small group of architects introduced a Néo-Grec style which, although it was itself shortlived, had a considerable influence on French art for a long time afterwards.

In England and in Germany towards the end of the eighteenth century there was a gradual replacement of the Roman Revival by the Greek Revival. There was a newly awakened interest in Attic art and in England there was a tendency to use Greek Doric and Ionic columns indiscriminately whatever the type of building, often without the carving and sculpture which should have accompanied them. However, the Greek style gained popular favour and improved in its design and execution until it finally gave way to the Victorian Gothic in about the middle of the nineteenth century. In Germany the Greek Revival was applied more rationally and was suitably modified to suit modern requirements.

There was little or no revival of either Roman or Greek in Italy. There were a few works in the late eighteenth and early nineteenth centuries which, built in the spirit of the late Renaissance, took from the revival of classicism elsewhere a greater correctness of detail rather than any change of form.

In Great Britain the Palladian style of Wren and Gibbs was continued until superseded by the Greek Revival, with a distinct tendency towards the classic Roman types. The Royal Exchange (1789) and the Mansion House (1739) were two examples of this Roman style. The Bank of England (1788) seems to have been the first example of the Greek idiom superseding the Roman. Sir John Soane seems to have copied the Greco-Roman order of the temple at Tivoli on a long low façade with a recessed colonnade. The British Museum, built about 1848, was almost pure Greek in style, with its Ionic colonnade which, being so large, cut off much light. The Fitzwilliam Museum at Cambridge was more successful, although it was just as Roman as it was Greek. Perhaps the most successful of the Greek designs were the porches of St George's Hall in Liverpool, although its hall and interior generally were Roman rather than Greek. The monuments to Robert Burns and Dugald Stewart were successful examples of Greek Revival minor works.

In Germany the classic revival followed Roman styles at first but the earliest example of Greek Revival was the Brandenburg Gate (1784) in Berlin. K. F. Schinkel (1781–1841) was instrumental in stimulating activity in the Greek style, although in his domed church of St Nicholas in Potsdam he utilized Roman forms, and followed the Renaissance in a few other buildings. He had a preference for the Greek and built the Old Museum in Berlin with a portico of eighteen Ionic columns. He also built the Court Theatre in Berlin.

Elsewhere there was not a great deal in the way of imitations or reproductions of Roman colonnades, although the church of S. Francesco de Paola in Naples, the Superga in Turin, the façade of the San Carlo Theatre in Naples and the Braccio Nuovo in the Vatican each came near to the style of the Roman Revival, although they all expressed some originality in their treatment. The University, the Museum and the Academy of Art and Science, all in Athens, were fairly successful examples of adapting Greek art to modern structures.

Peter the Great reigned in Russia from 1689 to 1725, and at about that time there was a varied mixture of architectural styles. Something like the style of the Jesuits in Italy modified to suit the Russian taste resulted in architecture like the later buildings of the Kremlin, and perhaps the not so extravagant Citadel Church and Smolnoy Monastery of Leningrad. There were also buildings of a more severe and classical type like the Greek Church in Leningrad, which had a Roman dome interior and a Greek Doric exterior. The greatest classic building, however, was the Cathedral of St Isaac in Leningrad. It had a dome of cast iron which was made to look like marble and Roman Corinthian colonnades with pediments projecting from its four sides. The Palace of the Grand Duke Michael reproduced the colonnades of the Garde Meuble in Paris on its garden front.

20
Victorian and Edwardian

There was great progress in mechanical, scientific and commercial activity during the nineteenth century. As a result, the standard of living generally improved and, with education, the energies of people were absorbed by pursuits which temporarily replaced the artistic creation of forms and objects which had occupied them in earlier ages. Nevertheless, the artistic spirit was not entirely lost and, after the middle of the nineteenth century, in architecture in particular, there was great progress. In France for a time popular taste stuck to the Renaissance with modifications, like the Néo-Grec, which broke the Roman tradition. About 1845, a few Gothic buildings of note were produced, which gave impetus to the study of medieval buildings. It resulted in a freer and more rational approach than had been the case under the classic designers, and examples of this included the churches of Ste Clothilde and of St Jean de Belleville in Paris, and the Bonsecours Church in Rouen. The church of St Augustin made use of iron and brick for its dome and vaulting and tile for external decoration. Iron was used increasingly for roof trusses and for the construction of markets and other commercial buildings, the Halles Centrales in Paris being an early example.

There was great architectural activity during the reign of Napoleon III (1852–70). The Louvre and the Tuileries were completed during this period. The New Opera was built about this time, as also was the Palais de l'Industrie built for the exhibition of 1855. Several railway stations in Paris which were largely constructed of iron and glass were examples of the modern French style Renaissance. The French were eminently successful in their construction of theatres, fountains and monuments which they completed in large numbers. The fountains of St Michel, Cuvier and Molière in Paris, and of Longchamps in Marseilles, illustrated the elegant detail of the French in this field. Napoleon III did much to improve the splendour of Paris and other cities by embellishing them with avenues and squares on a large scale.

After the fall of the Second Empire there was a tendency for French architecture to shed any traces of excess or eccentricity and to adopt a

153

more generally refined taste. During this period the Sacré Coeur Church in Montmartre, the École de Médecine and the Sorbonne were built. There was a definite attempt to be original and to discard traditional forms in the metal and glass exhibition buildings of 1878, 1889 and 1900.

In Germany and Austria there was a medieval revival partly accompanied and partly followed by the Greek Revival in Germany, a number of buildings were erected in the basilican, Romanesque and Gothic styles. These included the Aukirche in Munich, Gothic style, the Byzantine Ludwigskirche, also in Munich, and the Votive Church in Vienna (1856). The latter was reminiscent of St Ouen of Rouen and was of similar size and style to Ste Clothilde in Paris, and St Patrick's Cathedral, New York. The German theatres and concert halls which made free use of Renaissance and Classic forms were more successful than the churches. The Dresden Theatre and the Viktoria Theatre in Berlin should be noted. In Vienna the Opera House was built in 1861–69, and the Burgtheater was built in ornate Renaissance style.

Late in the nineteenth century Vienna underwent transformation. The entire centre was remodelled and magnificent boulevards and squares were created around a number of important buildings including the Parliament House and the Town Hall. The latter was Neo-Gothic and of great size. The University and Museums were in Renaissance style, which prevailed in the new city over the Classic or Gothic Revival.

Although in Great Britain the Anglo-Greek style was still in its infancy, there was an effort to revive the Anglo-Gothic, and in the period 1825–40 a number of buildings were completed in imitation of the Gothic with pointed arches and medieval buttresses. Later, with more experience, there came a more correct interpretation; and with the restoration of a number of medieval structures this resulted in a lack of any original development and merely a repetition of the old. It did, however, establish standards which improved church architecture.

For nearly three hundred years the tendency to achieve archaeological correctness held sway, but inevitably and slowly it gave way to an effort to adjust and adapt Gothic designs to up-to-date needs, instead of merely copying an out-of-date style. A number of leading architects were involved in this movement, including Sir Gilbert Scott, George Edmund Street, Alfred Waterhouse and William Burges. Perhaps the largest and most expensive of the structures built at this time was that of the Houses of Parliament at Westminster. Begun in 1839, it was perhaps the most successful of those built in the Victorian Gothic style. The architect was Sir Charles Barry. The Albert Memorial by Scott and the Law Courts by Street, both in London, were conscientious and careful designs but unsuited in style to their purpose, as was the Natural History Museum in South Kensington which was built in a modified Romanesque style. The church architecture was, in contrast to these other buildings, dignified and simple in design, and its good taste was worthy of special praise. It was by comparison highly successful.

As in the case of the Anglo-Greek, the Victorian-Gothic failed because of the difference between modern needs and medieval designs. From about 1860 there tended to be a return to the Renaissance style, and adaptations of this were seen in a number of buildings such as museums, colleges and town halls. The Imperial Institute, the Victoria and Albert Museum and the London County Council building, all in London, were examples. For a while Norman Shaw, Ernest George and others enjoyed a vogue in their Queen Anne style, and a number of mansions, schools and colleges were erected successfully in a type of Tudor-Gothic.

In releasing itself from archaeological revivals and improving in taste and in originality, British architecture made great strides forward. In other countries too there was exhibited in architectural design a greater freedom and improvement in taste, notably in France and Germany. In Italy there was tremendous building activity from about 1870 onwards. Among the structures of the time were the Monument to Victor Emanuel, the National Museum and the Palace of Justice, all in Rome.

Towards the end of the nineteenth century a movement began to show itself in France and Belgium which spread to Germany and Austria, and to a certain extent to England, which ignored the styles and traditions of the past with a preference for greater originality and a more personal style of decoration. It was a reaction against adhering to traditional methods and forms, and in fact was a protest against established traditions and ideas. This movement was called *L'Art Nouveau*. It resulted in great individuality and originality even to an extreme of eccentricity and bizarre extravagance, contrasting in range with a refined and reserved style. The least successful endeavours in this movement were in architecture, although there was real success in jewellery, silverware, vases and small furniture. The buildings tended to be stiff, eccentric or ugly. As in the case of Louis XV its greatest success was in small objects, furniture and interior decoration. L'Art Nouveau was well demonstrated in the buildings of the Paris Exhibition of 1900, in which the success of the clever and beautiful decorative details made up for the failure to improve upon the established building styles. L'Art Nouveau did achieve one important thing: it broke the hold that traditional classic design had held for so long, in favour of a more free and individual personal touch.

21
Architecture in the U.S.A.

When a country is first colonized, the people who settle there tend to bring with them as far as they can the habits and tastes of the old country. The new conditions with which they have to contend often force them to modify their ways and practices. Quite often the primitive nature of the new home, with its paucity of cultivation and civilized amenities, was in marked contrast to the activities and ideas of the colonists, and the struggle to bring some semblance of organized life out of chaos usually absorbed their energies for a considerable period, and prevented them from indulging in any form of cultural activity. In order to survive, they had to conquer nature, but when this was gradually achieved there was a growth in trade and in wealth, and the slow emergence of a cultivated class of people who had more leisure and time for culture. Initially, there was a tendency to reproduce the art of the mother country, but new conditions often imposed new developments on that traditional base. Commercial and cultural contacts with other lands brought in new influences which had some effect on the development of the still young colonial art. With political and economic independence and the development of resources and growth of a truly national culture, the arts grew and developed independently.

The early colonists in the United States of America did not build in stone. In the Southern and Dutch colonies the important buildings were mostly of brick, but wood was most commonly used. Wood frequently determined the form and style, but there was not much architectural elegance until the influence of Wren's work had some effect on the Middle and Southern colonies in the eighteenth century. Williamsburg Town Hall in Virginia and St Michael's Church in Charleston were attributed to Wren, but they had no special architectural elegance, although they were of simple and pleasing design.

During the period 1725–75 there was an increase in the building of churches and homes of the wealthy, with the growth in population along the coast. During this time the Colonial style developed, based on the architecture of the reigns of Queen Anne and of the two King

156

Georges in England, and in the case of churches on the style of Wren and Gibbs. Because wood was normally used, the details were inevitably subjected to modification. Internally, the refined treatment of the woodwork reflected the cultured taste of the local aristocracy. Stone structures were relatively few, and administrative buildings were not of any consequence because of lack of funds from the home government, and the poverty of the colonies.

The churches of this time included a number of interesting designs, among which were the Trinity Church in Newport, St Paul's in New York, which was actually built of stone in 1764, and also the first Baptist Church at Providence, Rhode Island. There were many churches worthy of note scattered through New England, Maryland and Virginia.

There were varying types of houses in the different colonies. Maryland and Virginia, for example, had a large number of brick manor houses in extensive walled grounds. Internally, these homes were elaborate and displayed a high standard of workmanship. Some examples included Westover and Carter's Grove, both built in 1737 in Virginia, and the Harwood and Chase houses of Annapolis, Maryland, built in 1770. The houses in New England were of wood and they were more compact; they did not have the stately air of the South, but they were more picturesque and varied in design. The interiors, both in New England and in the South, showed the same style in their stairs, mantelpieces, cornices and wainscots, and displayed an adaptation of classic forms to wood construction. Externally the orders were incorporated in porches and large pilasters, and Italian style windows. Doorways were elegant and of refined designs.

There were no large cities at this time; places like New York, Boston and Philadelphia were still little more than large villages, and their public buildings were of modest size and inexpensively built. Large monumental structures were as yet beyond the means of the colonists, and the greatest successes lay in their churches and houses which were all modest in size and not at all imposing or impressive.

In the latter part of the colonial period there were a number of interesting buildings erected during the Spanish rule in California, Florida and the South-West. These included Fort San Marco, renamed Fort Marion (1656–1756) and the Catholic Cathedral (1793), both in St Augustine, Florida.

When the colonies achieved independence and self-government and their resources rapidly increased, architecture took on a more monumental appearance. Stone began to be used generally, and domes, bell-towers and colonnades became features of civil architecture. The building of churches continued in the Wren-Gibbs style, but the classic forms became more correct. In the Connecticut Valley in Hartford and New Haven, Ithiel Town and Isaac Damon built a number of excellent churches. In the New York City Hall (1802-12) could be seen the influence of the style of Louis XVI. The Capitol at Washington (1793-1830), the State Houses at Boston (1795), Annapolis and Hartford (1812), the Virginia State House at Richmond and the University of Virginia, Charlottesville (1817) were examples of the classic influence of this period.

The influence of European classic revivals in the United States reached its peak in about 1830-40. The greatest impression it made was on government and civic buildings, although it also had some effect on domestic architecture in houses of wood and of brick, with Greek colonnades and porticos. The Greek Revival, reflecting the movement in England, began to displace the Roman in about 1820, and dominated public architecture for nearly thirty years. Important government buildings of this time included the Treasury and Patent Office buildings in Washington, the Customs House in Boston, and the Customs House in New York. Gerard College in Philadelphia (1847) was an imitation of a Corinthian Greco-Roman temple which was not perfectly adapted to its modern functions. The Capitol in Washington was greatly enlarged and wings were added with Corinthian Roman porticos. The Dome, which was added between 1858 and 1863, was of iron painted to look like marble. All in all, however, the Greek Revival in the U.S.A. was more successful than it was in Germany or in England.

From 1850 to 1870 there was great industrial growth and tremendous political activity. There were few buildings of architectural importance, however, during this time. The upheaval of the civil war, the building of the Pacific Railroad (1869) and the tremendous development of manufacturing, and mineral resources, all led to feverish commercial activity, but some stagnation in the arts. Perhaps the most notable achievement in architecture was St Patrick's Cathedral in New York. Trinity Church and Grace Church, though both of earlier date, were also worthy Gothic examples.

The building of the railways and the settling of people in new communities in the West, together with the industrial activity after the civil war, had a considerable effect on the artistic life of the country, which was enhanced by the tendency for people to travel to Europe. Schools of architecture were opened in Boston and some other cities, and art museums were opened or enlarged in New York, Boston, Philadelphia, Baltimore and elsewhere. Two architects who had been trained in the École des Beaux Arts in Paris, R. M. Hunt (1828–95) and H. H. Richardson (1838–86), did a great deal to stimulate public interest in architecture, and W. R. Ware did much to influence the pupils trained in the two architectural schools of Boston and New York.

The Centennial Exhibition of Philadelphia (1876) exposed the people of the United States to European and Oriental art in their own country for the first time. Its consequences were far-reaching; they extended from industrial and decorative art and rapidly spread to painting and architecture. Students began visiting the art centres of Europe in increasing numbers. Standards became higher at home and a number of art-industries were the fruits of this awakening of artistic interest. The Columbian Exhibition in Chicago in 1893 gave further impetus to the growth in interest in architecture.

The training of a large number of American architects in the École des Beaux Arts in Paris did not result in American architecture having a French style imposed upon it, because local conditions and materials and local taste militated against this. Some influence in monumental design was apparent but there was no imitation of French designs as such. The Gothic Revival, which lasted from 1840 to 1875, of which the State Capitol at Hartford Connecticut was an example, was generally made use of in church architecture, as in the cathedral in Albany, New York and St John the Divine in New York. Later works were generally in a style determined by the nature of the building itself and by the individual designing it and his training. There were many influences brought to bear on the style and design of each structure. Trinity Church, Boston, and the County Buildings at Pittsburgh executed in a free version of French Romanesque showed the strong individuality of Richardson, their designer, rather than the historic style he used.

The same could not be said, however, of many of his imitations. The Chicago Columbian Exhibition which made use of Renaissance forms and details resulted in the extinction of the French Romanesque, and from then on Renaissance styles prevailed. New materials and methods and different ideas all left their mark in planning and proportions irrespective of the styles used. The introduction of such things as the passenger lift or elevator as a substitute for staircases also had an influence.

New types of buildings had to be developed to fill a rapidly growing demand for well-lit offices, in places where the amount of space in a concentrated business area was very limited. This resulted in the erection of buildings of an exceptional height, constructed with a framework of steel columns and beams, filled in by walls. Some of the earliest of these tall buildings were the West Street Building, the American Surety Building, and the Metropolitan Life and Woolworth Buildings, all in New York. The last two were 700 feet (213 m) and 765 feet (233 m) high.

In the field of domestic architecture the varying climates have played no little part in the requirements of individuals in their houses. Often, for example, a broad staircase hall served as a family sitting room, while in a warmer climate a piazza or verandah met a real need. Planning tended to have regard to maximum convenience rather than to any particular traditional type. This resulted in exteriors arising from the interior arrangements rather than conforming to any particular style, and for comfort and luxury being striven for without regard to any particular monumental effect. However, a number of large town and country houses were built on a palatial scale in an elaborate manner, as in the cases of those of Vanderbilt, Reid, Carnegie and Schwab in New York. Later there was also a tendency to build to Colonial models, the style of which lent itself to the dignity and elegance to which large residences are suited, together with the elaborate landscape gardens which often went with them.

Generally speaking, American architects were never so successful with church architecture as they were with civic, and perhaps the preference for small parish churches interfered with the development of grander types of church buildings. Nevertheless there was some improvement, in which some churches either in Gothic or Neo-Classic had dignity and sound construction.

In the period 1880–90, there was a considerable advance in the beauty of detail and monumental effect, as in the Madison Square Garden in New York and the public libraries in Boston, New York, Pittsburgh and Washington. There was a new taste for monumental effects with dignified and appropriate detail, which brought architecture into closer union with all the allied arts, which included landscape gardening. With the development of steel frame construction came a transformation in commercial architecture, and a new interest in the planning of cities and the congestion of populations in them.

After 1900 architectural activity was not confined to industrial and commercial activities. While lofty office buildings in the commercial centres continued to be erected, educational buildings went up both in the East and in the West. As a result of an international competition, the design of an M. E. Bénard of Paris was selected for a grand group of buildings to be erected for the University of California. Columbia University and New York University, both in Neo-Classic style, were completed and many other universities or colleges added extensively to existing buildings or planned new buildings with new designs. Competitions for design awards for important public buildings resulted in a tremendous improvement in American architecture generally.

After 1900 there was a distinct movement in the United States for a general improvement in the cities by a replanning of the streets and squares and the embellishment of existing roads and squares with parks and boulevards. Successful replanning took place in many cities including Washington and Chicago. There was also a general improvement by the replacement of earlier buildings at Princeton, Yale, Chicago and John Hopkins Universities. These tended to be divided between a modernized Gothic and a return to Gothic.

22
Twentieth-Century
Architecture

To describe adequately the many styles and skills of twentieth-century architecture would require a book in itself in order to do it justice. In the last eighty years, the modern world has seen numerous styles come and go and interact with each other, as well as a large number of gifted architects, each of whom has contributed to the explosion of modern architectural ideas. In fact, it may be true to say that there have been more architectural styles created in this century than in the whole of the last two millennia. This is because of the rapid growth of industry and commerce, and the ever-rising standards of living of the general populace. This demand has given an opportunity to architects to invent and innovate, using materials which were not available to earlier generations of architects, but with which totally new concepts of structures could be created.

The age of plastics, concrete, aluminium and other almost exotic materials has produced both good and bad architecture. Where these modern materials have sought to imitate more traditional materials, the result has often ended in dismal failure. On the other hand, where architects have sought to use modern materials for their own sake, utilizing their own qualities, the results have been, in many cases, wildly spectacular and successful. Any study of architecture of the twentieth century must include an examination of twentieth-century structural engineering, for the two go hand in hand. Perhaps more than any other time in history buildings are now increasingly designed for specific purposes, whether residential, commercial, industrial, educational or for worship. The functionality of some of these buildings has often been criticized but, unlike any of the Victorian structures, twentieth-century edifices tend not to disguise their function but openly to advertise it.

Modern architectural styles generally know no national boundaries; thus it is possible to find fine examples of modern architecture throughout the world, even in the Third World. In fact, twentieth-century architecture has often stifled traditional styles with a blanket of modernity. Some of the greatest pieces of architecture of the twentieth-

The modern Roman Catholic Cathedral in Liverpool.

century include buildings by Le Corbusier and Perret (France), Berlage, Dudok, Mendelsohn, Mies van der Rohe and Gropius (Holland), Basil Spence and Lutyens (Britain), and Frank Lloyd Wright (United States). Brazil is probably one of the greatest monuments to twentieth-century tradition, with its cities Brasilia, Sao Paolo, Rio etc. full of fine examples of twentieth-century buildings.

There are so many good examples of architecture in the twentieth-century style that listing them would serve little purpose. It simply remains to be said that to find a good modern building simply look around you, for architecture is a living tradition, and new buildings of quality are constantly being erected in cities and towns throughout the world.

Index

The figures in **bold** refer to colour plates. Those in italics refer to the page numbers of black and white illustrations. Some important buildings are indexed under the name of the town or city in which they are situated.

167